FREQUENCIES

University of Utah Press Poetry Series

Other Titles in the Series

Days Going/Days Coming Back
Eleanor Ross Taylor
1991

Against Paradise
Jonathan Holden
1990

A Day at the Races
Sidney Burris
1989

Snow Water Cove
Jeannine Savard
1988

Headlong
James McKean
1987

Einstein's Brain
Richard Cecil
1986

Greenwich Mean Time
Adrien Stoutenburg
1979

GWEN HEAD

FREQUENCIES
A GAMUT OF POEMS

Berkeley
May 17, 1992

For Ben & Marlene,
dear friends, gentle readers
with love,
Gwen

UNIVERSITY OF UTAH PRESS SALT LAKE CITY 1992

University of Utah Press Poetry Series
Dave Smith, Editor

See Acknowledgments, page 140, for permissions statements

Many of the poems in FREQUENCIES first appeared in SPECIAL EFFECTS and THE TEN THOUSANDTH NIGHT, © 1975, 1979 by Gwen Head and first published by the University of Pittsburgh Press. Poems from these collections are designated in the text by the abbreviations *SE* and *TTTN* respectively.

∞ This symbol indicates books printed on paper that meets the minimum requirements of American National Standard for Information Services — Permanence of Paper for Printed Library Materials, ANSI A39.38–1984.

Library of Congress Cataloging-in-Publication Data

Head, Gwen, 1940–
Frequencies: a gamut of poems/Gwen Head.
p. cm. — (University of Utah Press poetry series)
ISBN 0-87480-395-0
I. Title. II. Series.
PS3558.E14F74 1992
811′.54 — dc20 91-51100
CIP

for Bernard and Katharine
and in loving memory
of my parents
Elsie Zaffarine Scott and Harry Gwen Head

CONTENTS

I. ". . . visible"

II. ". . . invisible"

I

"...VISIBLE"

BLOND MAHOGANY

They marry. The fashion is blond mahogany,
the wood of their parents' marriages glamorized:
the epic yoke of half a century
of getting and begetting, lightened in a chemical trice,
and love tweezered into a rainbow arch of amazements
that will never fall flat, or vanish into rain.

The year their belated daughter is born, the medallions
on head and footboards begin to pucker and glare
like wrinkled elbows. The tawny veneers start trying
to walk out on the pattern, as celluloid collar stays
avert their crispness from wilting shirts and bodies.
An edgy twilight condenses towards rain.

The family complete, they sleep in separate beds.
Twin beds. The gravitational droop of shoulders
and jowls attests the likeness, hard-won, asexual.
Under the blond mahogany headboard, their child,
trying to be two people, sleeps and wakes

in the dark, and the wood grain rises to the surface
in golden swirls and eddies, the streaming hair,
the opera cape, the pelt of the drowned girl
crouched naked at the keyhole of all dreams,
whose bruised eyes never open, but ooze salt
and green decay, and leave the pillow damp.

In what flood did she drown?
Can one live through such storms?

One night the rain shapes continents on the ceiling
and throbs in a gamelan of buckets and mixing bowls.
The walls shake with the racket of roundhouse turntables.
The windy streetcars crash to the end of the line,

and the two steal in, and lay them down to rest
in the trembling dark, beneath the invisible
and luminous wood, on either side of their child,
as if beneath a headstone, until she

becomes the hurricane's calm, seductive eye,
the wedding jewel clasped by jealous guards.

TOYS

Here are jewels, real jewels
in a blue glass jar.
The colors look pretty, mixed up like canned vegetables.
The diamonds have holes in the middle.
They are little, but best. They are patient
as doorknobs, they want the sun's dazzle
on the facets that scratch my fingers, glitter
that will be sand again someday.

* * *

These are the witch's spring colors,
too rare for wobbly eggs no one will eat,
or the sickly, sopping wet chicks.
In light they get ripe, they flood
the dusty planks with the vinegar smell of rainbows.
Real only when seen through, they still
can kill you.
When they meet like radio murderers, they turn black
like those mop-shaped fish — are they squid? —
that hide when they're frightened
in clouds of ink.

* * *

This one is a Marine, baby brother.
His khaki doesn't come off.
He's soft and blunt, a pillow boy.
But when I threw him, his face cracked.
That's sad, no one can love him now, though my mother
says we must try.

* * *

Too sweet all over to be touched.
If there were little windows
between *her* flowers, you'd see
rubber bands, springs, weights, dark like an attic.

Her hair can't come down now, she went to the beauty parlor.
It was sticky, then hard.

I had to thank a man I didn't like.
Her crown is pretty, her eyelids have black bristles.

But she can't point her toes like I can, or turn out right.

* * *

She's too big. But the little ones swim
in the shoebox full of cellophane.
Shirtboards make starchy white furniture
and a round laundry machine with a Scotch tape window.

But Jesus is best.
His beard and hair are brown, so I made the thorns
red like the hole in his side. You could run a string
through the ones in his hands and feet, that are big and flat
as paddles.
                    This is paper-doll clothes. The tabs
lift on and off. See, here's
that long thing that made mother angry.

PATIO PIECE

Escaping the dishpan
too white to hide in,
crossing a brown
desert of broadloom,
you paused on the landing, tasting
dust, and the distant tang of green;
then, whether resolute
or merely clumsy,
took the plunge,
skipped down twenty-eight
separate precipices
secure in yourself
as a shied stone,
and clattered to rest
in the courtyard
stove-up and jubilant.

In your melon stripes
with pinhead eyes
like plant lice,
you seemed at home
near the tepid water hole
watched by a drooling lion.
The banana trees
were tall as giraffes.
The queen's crown swarmed
over elephant ears
and alligator pears
like an army of pink ants.

The pale green
lapped plates
of your back made
a moist rosette
like the succulent hen-and-chickens.

Your accordion-pleated
ruff had unfolded
to full stretch
like a bellows, getting the picture.

But when I picked you up
the tendril legs
had lost their grip.
The belly shell,
unhinged, swung open
like the doors to a meat locker.
Your tail was stiff as a thorn.

I planted you
in the warm mud
under the stony
cairn of your shell,
aptly enameled
with the dim inscription
"souvenir," and the red
rose of extravagant love.

THE PRIZE

Acid-cured, the pages flake, fall away,
the color of bright Virginia.
Le Journal de Bord d'Alfred:
on page three, the family packs, in an uproar.
Toward the end, Maman falls ill, Jeannine learns to smoke.
But nothing explains the cover,
which, after forty-five years,
retains its mystery.

Alfred, in short pants,
lies propped on his elbows, scribbling.
In his left hand, a tooth-stitched apple.
Behind him, a giant, shiny cherry bomb.
Behind it, a white rabbit with cocked, flop ears.

The book's owner, too, is a mystery.
Ducking a curtsy
on an improvised stage
in the Ursulines' courtyard,
too shy to look at the principal
with her elegant upswept hairdo,
the six-year-old scholar, at that moment,
thinks for the first time
of suicide.

Can you pity her now, reader?
Or imagine how she envies
you, too clever to be taken in
by anything so foolish as a book?

COMING DOWN

(the Panhandle landscape near Amarillo, Texas)

The wagons came.
The grass fell away from their wheels.
But the ruts stayed.
The ruts have lasted for years.
From the air the ruts shine white on the brown cross-hatching
of the fields, the initials of lost
lovers ingrown in bark.
Where the fields peter out, there are canyons
and dry wash seen small
as lichens or dying moss, and in the canyons
the frail trees bend their shoulders to the wind
that harrows the staked plains now, that harrowed them then,
when the first wheels came.

The wheels are spinning.
The wheels are spinning still.
Two days out of sixty, glistening needles of water
eke out their meager circles. Hopeful grass
springs up beneath. Rows of green gauges
record the pressure of growth. Too soon the needles
waver and fall dry.
But the pumps still beat.
With tireless levers and pinions
they alight in the wake of a plenty receding, receding,
and day and night utter their scavenger cries.

The wagons have gone.
But all tracks stay and weather,
as the bones of an old skull
emerge from the failing flesh.
So now the green gauges darken, the pressure plummets,
the plundered vaults

of dolomite empty and echo,
and the hot heart of the earth shrinks in on itself,
and the earth wears its flayed skin smiling, brown and downy
as any child's cheek.

The airplane's shadow scissors and glides to rest,
before me the portal
of this garden, this paradise.

TEXAS

I.

Surrounded by the hushed
roar of air conditioning
we ride, as if in a monstrous
wheeled seashell.

Behind is a burnished
tunnel of dust, resembling
the tarnished barrel
of a telescope.
Its eyepiece frames,
in lieu of stars, a single
rusty grasshopper jigging
in place, patient as an ox.

This, I am told, is wealth,
as are the red lake
tangled in its thicket
of drowned mesquite
like a stopped heart
and the interminable muster
of ghost bushes
with their linty fruit.

Above us, noncommittal
buzzards are at rest
on the buoyant void, beat
after desultory beat.

We get out.
My old uncle staggers.
The heat jolts the back
of his throat like neat whiskey.

The foreman's garden contains
twelve gladioli, each
bound to a stake, each
of a different color.

Inside, in close-curtained dimness
an improbable broadloom meadow
is blooming. Its colors, like those
of fish netted at vast
depth, seep away unnoticed,
irrevocable. All stand
in a circle, shake hands, and whisper
of rain. Again of rain.
Always of rain.

Going home, they have to stop
the car and open the door
for me. Not knowing why,
I lean out, vomit furiously
on the insistent dust.

II.

The unseen child
in the attic room
with dormer windows like
abandoned dollhouses,
sleeps, jerking in fever,
like a bucking pony.

Silent, the mother comes,
her nightdress defiantly
white as a freshwater pearl.
Her lips move. An angry
buzzing fills the room.
The windows go black
and like a plague of locusts
the rain falls.

FIRST BLOOD

Though I speak with the tongues
of men and of angels

We perched like starlings
on a grid of folding
chairs in the gymnasium.

I am become as sounding brass
or tinkling cymbals

After the reading
before the hymn
we were told the news.

A mighty fortress is our God

As we sang all heads
turned to your empty seat
its flimsy metal
provisional, apologetic,

A bulwark never failing

and it was as if
you had won some prize.

— equal to the sum
of the squares of the two sides

The radiators squealed and farted.
On each divider
of my notebook I drew
a fluent, many-tendriled cartouche
enclosing nothing.

"You're noan so far
fro' Thornfield now"

All day in my mind the door
of your familiar comfortable house
opened and shut like the jaws
of the whale.

No grandeur to overwhelm
no stateliness to embarrass

Under the chapped skin
of my cold hands
subterranean rivers
of blood were flowing.

Nox est perpetua una dormienda
The seconds spattered down like sleet.

Deinde centum, dein mille altera
Your young father below ground by nightfall.

AT THE PIANO

I.

Hunchback
minotaur
squared off
on black goat feet
tight-lipped, eyeless, mute —
you are cornered.
Now
I will fold you back like a quilt.
You will grin
like a glad foolish hound.
At my touch
your hollow flank
will buzz like a great golden hive
and all the stinging swarms rush out
singing their unknown language.

II.

The keys rise to my fingers
like diving boards
like the pliant stems of flowers
like necks bared to the axe
like the stairways of crumbling cities
like masses of candelabra
like the pits of ripe fruit.

They frolic like minnows.
They lie down like mild lambs.
They arch their necks like zebras.
They snap their beaks like macaws.
They are ponderous as the elephant
delicate as the garter snake
furious as the black swan.

I rejoice in their many lives.
We are one, well-knit
as a barrel hoop,
the perfect, gravity-defying round
through which the sun leaps.

MY GRANDMOTHER GARDENS

They were leeches on her, drew her blood like tides,
that hardy lady, camped upon her field chair
surveying the heavy charge of yellow roses,
bold cockscomb, and the janizary lilies;
loathing all blue and cloistered beautiful hours,
hot for the fierce flower, the short and lovely prime
of the morning glory, its trumpets flaring in valor,
or the musketry of salvia, rattling brigades
whose bright exemplars loomed, impaled like standards.

There she had sown them, dragon's teeth, bones of her mother,
bedded down soft to rend her with their carnage.
Canute, she seemed, of the sun, defying its round;
heliotrope, with cypress at her shoulder.

THE WOMAN IN THE MIDDLE

Begin with the heroine standing on a staircase,
three yards of tapered rose point slung from her shoulders,
in mandatory pearls, stephanotis,
and baby's breath, poised like a white bat.

Above her silken knees, the satin hem
hangs like a blade. It's nineteen twenty-nine.
In steamer trunks beneath the porte cochère,
the trousseau purchased on her grand tour.
Patou: a blue brocade with silver lace,
its bugle beads like regimented rain.
Embroidered black and white Chinese pajamas
to wear in the evenings, playing dominoes.
Teddies and step-ins, ostrich fans. To read,
Tristram and *Sonnets to a Red-Haired Lady.*
To flirt with, a long cigarette holder of
the first green plastic made to look like jade.
His gifts, by which we know across the years
that the groom is poor, but has a good heart.

Twenty-five years later his heart has given out.
Their daughter (a menopausal accident)
is old enough to count him up the stairs.
In steel-rimmed glasses, braces on her teeth,
her busy cranium's wired like a champagne cork.
One, two, three, . . . at ten, another step.
Her scrawny shoulder blades protrude like wings.

The heroine listens, rises — no it can't be!
Hose at the knees, flesh at the waist, hair
at the nape all rolled and tied or netted down,
and all an anonymous, shabby package color,
all with the slack sway and thump of the sleeper berth.

Can't be, but is.
                    This is her dressing table:
desk calendar with six weeks left unturned,
rings of spilt powder, piles of unanswered letters,
and a sealed bottle of *Je Reviens.*
Stabbing the pins into her hair, she goes
to thread a needle for her dragon mother.

What happened in the middle? Mother, tell me!
I'm in the middle now. Why wasn't there
a lover and a train to throw herself under,
in a last display of the pyrotechnic hair?

Or is this the train, this slow freight of years,
these sodden comforts of the hobo jungle?

THE DAY OF THE DEBUTANTE TEA

The day of the debutante tea, the exterminator
came in the early morning with fog and spray
and smoke to stink the skunks from under the house
where they lived in a lair of ducts and intricate brick
and fed the air we breathed with their wild perfume.
They were civil skunks; had never attacked direct,
but stank, as it were, at second hand, and stuck
at eviction. We chased the reek from room to room
as they hid themselves in our metal catacombs.
The pest man cursed a moment; sent us down
to the furnace room as beaters, that the din
might drive his quarry out as they came in.
And he met them with a shotgun; where it showered,
bloody bouquets of fur and sinew flowered
and died in a furious reek beneath the stair.
Their epitaph hung foul upon the air.

The stench endured; that day the house grew strange.
Like myriad ants the tarnish colonized
the oval glass whose cindered cyclops eye
took in the fallow corners of the ceiling
where cobwebs rioted like Queen Anne's lace.
And rampant on cool tile beneath the stair
basked scorpions. It was their shadows grew
like agate fossils in her lungs and brain.
At night opossums nattered on the roof.
My mother felt her bones prick at the flesh.
Nothing she knew but grew, furred, frayed, turned color,
slimed, gnawed, those days, until she knew no more
and kind men in white coats took her away.
By the cool drip from the bottle above her head
and the warm drip to the bottle beneath her bed,
she wasted from water to water like a stone.
They trellised tubes upon her, rooted her,
frail rhizome, on that white and sterile ground
where all grew plain; her final knowledge why
it felt at last so clean a thing to die.

UPHEAVAL

I woke in a fun house; found my living room
a box of veering parallelograms
like the bellows of an accordion. The floor
like a berserk teeter-totter lurched and dived.
Projectile treasures hurled themselves upon me:
a telescope, a Christmas candle. The armoire
opened its doors like a brown bear to crush me.
Forked lightning bit the plaster, and the beams
cracked out like rifle shots. The garbage cans
racketed in the alley. In the din
I rode like a sea-drunk sailor, feet set wide,
and thought amazed "That's God's voice. Things will change."

But nothing did. The mountains looked the same.
The city had landed catlike on its feet.
The carpenters banged at walls. The telephone lineman
put up his yellow parasol. At ten
the postman came. McCloskey walked his poodle.

But there were signs. In the quotidian
brown paper lunch bags, thermos jugs of coffee
still jigged unseen and broke out in shivering targets.
The strata, geologists said, were yanked askew
like a stack of books with one taken from the bottom.
Roots groped for another hold. The punctual branches
began to swivel back to their sundial stance,
and the mosses knit themselves together again.

But none of it showed. My altered skeleton
retained its balance, and my altered mind
thought customary thoughts. Although the old
shoe pinched a different toe, there was no saving grace.
The face in the mirror was a mortal face.

SE

MINUS TIDE

The water lunges
at the unseen moon.
Its glass doors slide back
revealing a range
of rock and brick, crowned
with the extinct cones of barnacles.
With each wave
the blue teeth of mussels
mesh and grind.
One heron hunches
above his reflection,
his shape a treble clef.

At the height of my reaching
fingertips, waves
have chopped a cliff, sheer
as iceberg or freeway
abutment. Horizontal,
a fallen laurel does push-ups
above the loose meander
of salt water. Tart
and coy, blackberries
drowse behind a portcullis
of thorns; their form, *morula*,
embryonic, bloody.

Among them, fireweed
bearded with white
floss that explodes
in jets of clinging filaments,
and hangs the sky
with a light mail
of airy linkages, a system
of pale neurons groping toward synapse.

SURE THING

for Katharine

Your father picked a filly from the paddock:
silver, insolent, an early fern
rearing above drab leaves; pliant as grass,
fickle as water, dappled like a streambed.
Mounted, she was a lethal blue machine.
Sure thing, he said.
                                        Driving through mud at the rail
the dirty wave sucked her under, head over heels
and held her, mauled her, teased her. When she surfaced,
riderless, on three legs, the fourth hoof dangled
on its chains of tendon, scattering blood like a censer.
Two men at her bridle, two at her stirrup, she would not
have done with running, but, bearing them all, waltzed
for home until the master rapped three times for silence.

Hers was a short dash and a quick ending.
I can no longer die young. The deepening lines
in my face, my palms, converge in perspective, forming
in my mind, as in an etching of Piranesi,
a baroque monument called Patience. Those long months
I carried you, I learned one lesson well:
First be a good animal.

WATER BABIES

The locker room floor
is slippery with banana peels.
Its talcumed air
is the air of a guano island.
From this port the mothers embark,
majestic of beam, tugged
by the young they will shortly cast off.

And now they are the shores of the one continent
from which all histories, great and small,
break loose and drift.
What waves of bawling crash against their ears!
They smile, they croon to the voyagers
who lie thrashing, eyes pinched shut,
in the glassy isolation of water,
a squared-off second amnion in which chlorine
cancels the essential salt.
Fragrant, far, merciless,
the spice islands of origin
step back and back, impregnable
behind the flowering atolls of their bathing dresses.

Still, water connects them, kinked
and pulsing. Mutual wrath
drives the fat pistons, sets
the infantile engines hooting like calliopes.
Theirs is the first fury. Gasping, bellicose,
through breaking waves they burst upon the world.

DEATH AND THE MAIDEN

The irises we bought
to gentle the coming
of unwelcome guests
are wet and ropy
as chewing gum, petals
rolled on themselves like stockings.

I snap them out
of their sockets like string beans.
Heaped in an ashtray
they are the soiled
linen of spring.
You gather them up.
"I am a bride," you say.
"This is my bouquet."

You march to the window,
command me to open,
and one by one lay them
on the kinky green moss,
among the torn red tulip petals,
of our window boxes
as if making a wager.

In a dawn gray
as spider web
I watch at the window.
The petals cling and shiver,
wet butterflies.
All is dissolved in rain.
This is a reluctant spring
and you are long asleep.

SE

FAIRY TALE

I keep thinking of the illustration
of a fairy tale I have forgotten,
its title some strange female name
full of grinding consonants,

and I would say that the picture sat above it like
an admonishing angel on a tombstone,
except that the creature's body
is left to the reader's imagination.

We see only the head
of a dead girl crowned with flowers.
She is not wearing
her petaled skin anymore
or the beckoning blue of her eyes.
Only the stone ramparts
of exemplary beauty remain:
snubbed septum, geared junctures
of fontanel and jawbone,
long hair — not honeyed, but glaring yellow floss —
and intact teeth, blandly murderous.

Yet she is familiarly horrible.
Even the jellied maggots
that course the chalky tear channels
are fat with the smugness of homily.

No, what terrifies
is the bodies we are not shown, they
and the perverse freshness
of the flowers.

Each day someone must gather the razor-petaled
gentians, and the daisies,
each with its golden core
of throttled trumpets.
                                        And someone
like a sad hound guarding a sacked arsenal,
each night, among thigh-swords, rib-knives,
smashed hauberks of breastbone and pelvis,
must lay down his hot life, his stubbornly
grieving and craving body.

SLIDE

Mahogany, teak, brass, a clipper ship
leans like a wind vane. Its rigging screams typhoon.
Inflamed and fleshy, sails, clouds, waves like Rubens
nymphs dismembered, struggle and subside.
It is a jigsaw puzzle. The pieces are scattered
on a green game table. They are shaped like irises.

Four women, three children, a man in a blue shirt
with a camera, have turned their backs. They are drinking beer
on the green madonna oval. They may founder
and drown in a tsunami of bloom if the wind rises.

They are watching the Steller's jay. Already, exact and blue,
he has snapped into a branch like a fan closing.
In a blur like falling water their fingers are heavy,
larval, and white. Their smiles are melting like ice cream.

One child has a red ball. One woman is sad.
Her proudest words, at four, were *ornate* and *precarious*.

A MUSICAL OFFERING

for Marvin McGee

I.

At Christmas, your telegram:
I love you. I've lost
your telephone number. No one
else gives me such presents, although
I can't remember now
what, when I called you, we said.

II.

The nearer I came to my native city, the more frequent
were the letters from my father. I therefore hurried forward
as fast as I could, although myself far from well.
My mother's disease was consumption. Seven weeks ago she died.
Ah, who was happier than I when I could still
utter the sweet name, mother, and it was heard?
And to whom can I say it now?
I have passed
very few pleasant moments since my arrival here.
To the asthma which I fear may develop
into consumption is added melancholy,
as great an evil as my malady itself.
In Augsburg you lent me three carolins, but I
must entreat for a time your indulgence.
My journey cost me a great deal, and I have not
the smallest hopes of earning anything here.
Fate is not propitious to me here in Bonn.
Pardon my chatter; it was necessary
for my justification.
I am, with the greatest respect,
your most obedient servant and friend —
Here,
on page eighty-nine, sunk in my own life,
I abandoned Beethoven, and since have read no more,
nor played his music, nor written to you.

III.

In the dark house, all that remains
is a gas log on the stone hearth,
two brass urns in leaded window niches
through which the blue day shines,
and a grand piano.
                                        A girl raises the lid,
sits down, and plays
a Bach partita. There is pure, airborne order.
The room lights up with blue butterflies.

A moment only. Her fingers stammer and stop.
The wings clap shut. The thread of music snaps.
Patiently she goes back, repeats, pieces together
the broken ends. There is a way out
of the dark house. She must have the wit to play it.

IV.

Last year I sent my piano,
older than I, younger
by far than you, away to be rebuilt.
Where it stood, the percussion marks
of my pedal heel overlapped
like ragged valves, at the top
of a lopsided heart outlined in yellow varnish.

Pianos age as we do.
The soundboard, that heartwood,
dries with time into its glory.
Cellulose, lignin, its ranks
of vegetable pipes hum at the least touch.

But the metal plate, under tons
of deep-sea pressure, buckles
and sags like a sunk galleon.
The rigged strings go slack.

Bits of wire and felt
sprout like hair in odd places.
The machine, in short, decays. The singing voice
falters, damped by excessive tolerances.

But now, what a comeback!
Copper strings like store teeth,
a giant clipspring bolted into the belly,
(that curve more tender than any living flank),
and the huge, shifty voice of a ventriloquist.

My cyborg, my pony, I don't know you,
with your face-lift and your megaphone, mysterious
as all my old friends.

V.

Heartbroken when the Great War began,
old La Pérouse stopped eating. Gide found his piano teacher
in a threadbare velvet armchair, not wanting to die
in the bed he shared with his termagant wife. The shutters
were almost closed. Imagine that dark room
with its senile clutter: a pile of hatboxes;
a bureau covered with uncut books; a garbage can
full of worn-out shoes; a dozen spirit lamps,
lit and unlit, like random votive lights;
untouched glasses of cider, and flies circling
loud in the August heat. The old man's face
was parchment white, spattered with the confetti
of age, fever, chagrin. Picture his mouth,
flabby and toothless, working its cud of grief.

Gide slipped him swallows of cider and sips of broth
each time he paused between injuries. Then he eased him
to his feet, found his hat, and helped him downstairs.

So the man who had written *The Immoralist*
and the old musician went their ways: La Pérouse
to his café, while Gide, unable to write,
played Bach all day, "preferring," he noted later,
"the fugues with a joyful rhythm," though the war went on.

Retelling this fable, I think of you and am comforted.

VI.

Old man, I beg you, do not
die yet. Teach me again
the art of things done badly
for love.

(Section II is a free condensation and paraphrase of a letter quoted in Thayer's Life of Beethoven, *revised and edited by Elliott Forbes, Princeton, 1967.)*

THE JAYS

Intending to praise their colors
I had prepared a palette
of cobalt, lapis, lignite, dragonfly.
It sat oddly on their ku-klux profiles,
their gaudy flamenco feathers.
They are most unnatural birds,
their true colors flashy,
trashy, meretricious,
like hydroplanes, pinball machines, vinyl motorcycle seats,
bowling balls, and the kind of Christmas tree lights
made in Japan and implicated
often in suburban holocausts.
Even their hideous cries are canned
like the hoarse quarrels on the daytime soaps.

I had intended to praise their fidelity,
but it seems they have no choice;
find each other so unlovable
that once met and mated
they hang together by centripetal force,
a furious blue binary star;
and even at rest, fan
their vexatious tails lightly, tirelessly
in the gambler's gesture, scanning
for the one winning hand.

Nor can I praise their indiscriminate appetites.
These are rare birds, able to swallow
anything to stay together,
gullets straining like the carnival geeks
who dine on swords, flame,
tin cans, wineglasses, nails;
and with bursting chests, throats
full of broken glass and blood,
celebrate unceasingly
their calamitous gift.

After ten years together
I make you a present of them.
Not praise.
But fact.

FRUIT OF THE SEASON

The cripple with his sack
of groceries moves
like a glacier with joints.
He passes two men
on the sidewalk digging
foxholes for weeping cherries.
His steps are calibrated,
minute, inexorable,
a flood gauge rising.

He has had enough of this pink snow
and thinks instead
of that bizarre diary
in which the tale is recounted
of an elegant banquet
in ancient China
at which the delicate brains
of living monkeys
were consumed as a first course,
these being trepanned at table
like soft-boiled eggs
and scooped out with enameled spoons;

thinks further of the great lady
who, finding herself old one day, remarked
"I no longer wish to make love,
only friendship."

QUEEN CONCHES

You and I strolled by the sea.
The offshore scrims of sunset
rustled meekly into place.
The sand was studded with conch shells,
cabbage-sized, bony parodies of the clouds.
You picked one up.
It was knobby, moist, foolishly
pink, the skull of a newborn,
only one small chink
an unclosed fontanel
above the chubby protrusions.
We, I have forgotten to mention,
were lovely, sensual, younger,
anointed with sunblock and insect repellent.

Of course we took it home with us,
strumpet shell, trollop shell, replica
of Balzac's boudoir,
its stone damasks and cashmeres
spread always in welcome.
Little horns, ravished operculum,
pouting, pearly nether lip —
we relegated it, and rightly,
to the bedroom.

There is another shell where I work,
the gift of a charter boat skipper down on his luck.
All its cotton candy is licked away,
its silken floss spun out.
What remains is a conspiracy
of little windows that scatter the light into lace.
What remains is the sea
itself in a winding sheet.

Over it, corals
lift shattered candelabra.
What remains is a hard-bitten diagram
of ruin, its spiral an ever-
evolving, ever-enlarging cul de sac.
This shape fits my hand like a weapon.

A naturalist might note
that shells are exoskeletons;
a moralist, that both of my shells
began as shelter.

LIFE MASK

I.

Only my face takes the plunge,
smeared with a channel swimmer's grease.
Long pig, I am served up on a trestle.

"We need your chin up."
I am given a roll of toilet paper for a neck pillow.
The single-handed applause
of the batter bowl rewards me.

"You'll feel some heat at first."
Now I am poured and spatulaed.
Yeastily I bubble through my nose hole
while the weight of plaster lies, smoothing me out.
Eyes clenched, lips taut, I wait
for the cold kiss of permanence.

It comes. The mask sucks and pops, pulling away.
I'm the first pickle from a fresh jar.
Watched over by ceramic trolls, I rise
from my hard bed, postoperative,
and try my earth legs, ashy
with the dust of making.

II.

"— the longest eyelashes —"
Fossils, they have embedded themselves in plaster,
meshed rows of bulrushes,
the eyeballs hidden baskets.
The sculptress tosses clay like pizza dough.
Earthy, aqueous, willful, her medium
slides down the nose chute,
stagnates in eye sockets.

Into the sterile furrow of the lips
the clay is tamped, patted, smoothed.
Between press and probing hand, a semblance
of flesh takes shape.
The packed mold is inscrutable as a thunder egg.

Meanwhile, behind the monocular
turret of her camera, the model
prowls, shooting. A nameless gray day
eyes her through the skylight.
Leaving, she will commend
this dream to the furnace: a self
all congealed flame, crystalline,
jagged.

III.

The box says PURE OLD-FASHIONED PEANUT BUTTER.
Inside, two lumpish versions of myself.
One is a somnambulist whose broken eyes
stare beneath stone awnings from an unclimbable tower.
The almost recognizable other, prognathous,
takes things as they come, on the chin.
Her hair is rendered in rubbery bathing cap waves.
Grimacing, she surfaces again, eyes gritted shut,
themselves the jaws of traps behind which
some endless, secret gnawing toward freedom occurs.

And indeed the smell of the thing when I lift and hold it
is unbearable: acrid, metallic,
a taint of dried blood.

A MARRIED COURTESAN

After ortolans, venison, grapes, Païva rose
groaning from a groaning table to indulge
his rarest taste, taking guests to see his wife,
his best excess, proudest surfeit, splendidly cumbered
in wig and petticoats, a captive comet
tricked out in gold brocade, two gross cabochons
stuck winking in her skull, bobbing in slow
somersaults, head over heels, in graceful orbit
forever in her formaldehyde aquarium.

A good wife rewarded, making daily rounds
in perfect glory, perfectly at ease.
She had been diligent in seduction, weaving
on cold eminence an artifice of thorns to win him,
opening to him alone, who scorned plain value,
craving extreme dragons and dangers. If at length,
grown weary in her cold tower, she fell asleep,
she must not be blamed. Grace is of iron;
locks on the flesh that wears it, and bites deep,
and takes the breath away. All perfect beauties sleep.

CIRCE

(A poem in the manner of the fruit
and vegetable portraits of Arcimboldo)

The wind grinds its teeth. A sleepless moon
floats in a sea of purple lees and whey.
In a snarl of tendril tails and flap ears,
ripe backs bulging like gourds, the pigs wait for their queen.
Their delicate trotters pinch the silken mud,
trying its texture. Intelligent and mean,
their black eyes swarm over her like aphids.

Bare feet precise as mattocks, she advances
through a meadow blue with chicory and forget-me-nots.
She wears a gown of thin and luminous onionskin.
Her hair is a rumpled cataract of fennel.

Lady of gardens, she offers up her burdens,
lets them devour the shapes they have made their own:
garlands of shaved peel, cushions of pulp, mounds
and ruffles of crisp and moist, the bitter rind
and grimy roots of her being, forked and swollen.

All, down to the shriveled and lethal kernel,
final, adamant, ominous as bone
she tenders her lovers, mistress of sty, kennel,
and lair, sum of her offerings, slut queen.

THE HAWK IN THE GARDEN

Looking out on a tidal
bore of *pieris japonica*
wreathed in plum blossom spray,
and beyond, a parade of canonical
lavender rhododendrons, and brave
crimson azaleas, hieratic
and protective, it seems my friend today
is a Doge come in his bridal
barge to cast his heart upon the waves
of a sea grown tiny, green, and emblematic.

But for this winged
memento mori
the color of a scab
or a piece of the True
Cross, this ripsaw-hackled
hawk, that in shackles,
brandishes her arsenal of drab
plumes, dark as if singed
in some more blinding glory,
and so undoes my story
that all I can do

is linger over coffee and gaze
appalled through the leaded panes.
Each beveled prism
cants the sane
morning light into
shards of rainbow. Dazed
I begin to
see the most innocent garden as a maze;
at its heart, dark stain
and unhealable schism.

SE

THE GARDENER'S DAUGHTER

In the plastic-shrouded
mop bucket, shriveled
cherry twigs, prickly
as barbed wire, wear
new shreds of bloom, and from

the lacquered tombs
of stale red beans
dynasties of gleaming jade trinkets
have been rifled and scattered.

My root bin is ravished,
my spice rack vandalized.
The angelic crests of decapitated carrots
watch over me as I dry
my dishwasher hands on air,

for the paper towels are all folded and fled
the saucers prestidigitated away
and on them sleep manifold tubers, cuttings, and pods.

My maiden daughter, gravid with the mad joy
of growing things, craves of me kiwi fruit,
papaya, pineapple, mango, cantaloupe, quince,
sesame, ginger, coriander, daikon
radish, and the waxen bells
of paper cups by the hundreds,
to set them humming with the clappers of roots
as the rattling seed covers split wide,

while above the red clay rim
of a pot, of the year, of the world,
last fall's withered, fragrant
yellow quince rises

and where now is winter?

For next to it
on the window sill
the pomegranate
stone apple   all seeds
sets ajar a mysterious
bronze portal, blue
with a patina of mold

and my child comes toward me
with the cloven fruit in her hand.

RAIN

Rain is the original stereotype,
billions of identical units, each intent
on the din of its own tiny bit of information:
about ice crystals, say, at forty thousand feet,
wind shear, or the pollen count
on the Siberian tundra.

It begins like a sprung nerve, twitching.
An invisible junco lands
on the laurel. Then a flock of them.
Something plays the ferns like a marimba.
It continues, in Satie's directions, *monotonously*, *whitely* —
like a nightingale with a toothache.
But this is more accurately rodent weather:
a clatter of nails and tail-tips on roof and walls,
the sour smell of a sickroom,
fear of bites while sleeping.

Awake and needing something, I go downtown.
Rain draws the maimed in thunderous masses
out into the slick streets as if to a shrine.
The dwarfs, the obese, the amputees, the mumblers, the dropsical
old women whose feet would make fine umbrella stands
crowd stupefied beneath the gray fountain
to be healed or drown,

and my taxi driver, taking a wrong turn, asks, "Lady
why do you look so sad?
You must be some kind of artist."

SLUG

How can he dare to cross me,
this oozing, footless tube,
lifting his alert pronged head
in the cuckold's gesture?

Long ago his nation
cast off the security of shells
and now go proudly naked
relying for safety
on the *realpolitik*
of sheer slug numbers.

Clearly he glories
in each nuance of slug calligraphy,
those sly paths of silver
that chronicle the progress
of appetite, and answer
the urgent appeals of the rain.

Perhaps he incarnates
the slug king of legend
who lay for seven days and seven nights
besotted in a saucer of beer
but did not drown

and who, by this test,
won his dappled queen
and with her dangled upside down
on a glittering rope
of commingled slime
convulsed and tranquil
as a hypnotist's pendulum.

Then together they passed
through the exorcist's circles
of slug bait unharmed
and will feast forever
on trilliums and tulips

if I choose to stay my foot.

I don't, but stand a moment musing,
their sticky deaths the mucilage
holding me earthbound
by all that is at once

most vulnerable
most destructive.

DREAD

In Muybridge's world, each creature,
biped or quadruped,
runs its single course unimpeded.
Clocked, segmented,
the frames slap into place:
railroad ties, a game of patience.

Actions flow out of each other.
The future bursts
from the ruptured cell wall.
Each motion, ambling or violent,
unfolds, ebbs, returns
in the simple tripartite pattern
of songs or flowers.
And the light is so spacious, so ripe.
Moving cornucopias, still lives
of globe and piston, toothsome,
ramshackle, spill from these pages.

The dog grins, tongue slack in the spanking breeze.
The eagle splashes black feathers over graph paper.
The elephant's loose skin flows and sparkles.
We forget that lives collide,
that those not running are fighting.

One card is always missing.
The locomotive bears down.
A melody lies asphyxiated on the page,
wings flattened, pins through the thorax.

A hidden cell detonates, goes dark.
Somewhere a young man weeps, embracing his wife,
and the mastiff Dread springs gaily.

The witty hinges and pivots
of his jaws sweep and gnash,
and a cat shreds into gobbets of bloody flesh.
Her furious hackles drift and settle like thistledown.

And somewhere my hand traces these words, warding off
the points and shears that with each frame draw closer.

THE SWANS OF SAIGON

Why does he have to talk to me,
this man in the secondhand duffel coat,
and what can I say to him?
He is wearing a watch cap and gloves,

this man in the secondhand duffel coat —
he keeps them on, though it's warm in here,
the watch cap and gloves he's wearing,
while we watch the nine-year-old dancers.

He sat down, without asking, beside me.
Now sidelong he scans my *New Yorker*,
then watches the nine-year-old dancers,
his eyes and his lips intent.

Sidelong he scans my *New Yorker*.
He is determined to talk to me.
His eyes and his lips are intent on it.
The first word that comes is *Saigon*.

He is determined to talk to me.
We fumble toward a common speech.
The first word that comes is *Saigon*,
French the one language we share.

We fumble toward a common speech.
My daughter is a swan queen in training.
The language we share is French.
Saigon était une très belle ville. . . .

My daughter is a swan queen in training,
though her prince is the plump instructress.
Saigon était une si belle ville. . . .
Now she is soaring, she smiles.

Her prince is the plump instructress.
The mirrors adore her frail limbs.
She is smiling, now, she is soaring.
Que faites-vous maintenant?

The mirrors adore her frail limbs.
He is trying to learn the language.
Que faites-vous maintenant?
He is washing dishes in Chinatown

while he tries to learn the language.
And what is it that *I* do,
while he washes dishes in Chinatown?
I tell him I have a daughter.

But what is it that I *do*?
I tell him I am a poet.
I tell him I have a daughter,
that my daughter is one of the dancers.

I tell him I am a poet.
But have I no other children?
My daughter is one of the dancers.
She is pale and fiery as moonlight.

But have I only *one* child?
Mes poèmes sont mes autres enfants.
She is pale, fiery as moonlight.
We have run out of conversation.

My poems are my other children.
How stupid we are with strangers!
We have run out of conversation.
He turns. He gets up to go.

How stupid we are with strangers. . . .
The swan children, too, are leaving
as he turns and gets up to go.
Moi, j'avais cinq enfants . . .

The swan children, too, are leaving.
He used a past tense of *avoir*:
Moi, j'avais *cinq enfants.*
He takes off his glove to shake hands.

In the imperfect tense of *avoir*
the past repeats and continues.
He takes off a glove to shake hands.
The skin is seared, bald ponyskin.

The past repeats, continues:
five soaring, flame-white swans . . .
His skin is seared bald ponyskin.
Why did he have to talk to me?

Soaring, flame-white swan children . . .
My daughter has lost one sock.
Why did he have to talk to me?
What can I say to him?

NOT SLEEPING

It is always too cold or too hot.
Like docile servants bearing
late mail, cold tea, the little
ills of the body announce themselves
and are naggingly present, friendly
when you would have them silent. Meanwhile
your mind plays all the wrong records, and a far
gate bangs in the wind.

In any house there are rooms for not sleeping.
Wakeful, you can do almost anything:
wax the floor until it gleams like a skating rink,
pay your bills, evolve a philosophy,
eat all the leftovers, water your plants, contemplate
the worsening world situation.
Unless you live alone, no music
except what you can read silently from score,
though if light-footed you may dance a little
or look in on your loved ones sleeping.

If these fail, move on.
Take a long drive, tracing the line
of some coast or other. Find
a new town, a late bar, a stranger's
bed, in which to lie wakeful
while far off some balky engine chugs and whines
and the gate goes on banging in your mind.

Still, courage. Nothing is more certain
than that, whether by stealth or by force
with or without your knowledge and consent
when you most expect it
when you least expect it
whether you think it is time or no
the wind will subside
the gate flop shut like a hymnal

and sleep will come.

DEATH IS LIGHT AS A FEATHER, DUTY IS HEAVY AS A STONE

Heavy with holding back
the taut arm falls like an axe.
The stone I am springs to you.

A sling of northering geese
when the cold fails, etch on blue
the same vast whistle of release.

Ashore, the sun-struck boulevards buckle and swell.
Coming from dark the sunlight stings like shrapnel.
I hurtle down your whistling in a barrel.

It's sound, but smells of peril.
Once when I was sick with our old quarrels
and balked to death, you brought me back, calling

that deaf, black wall *beauty.*
Lightened, I give you back your proverb. Duty
and death alike go lightly, each of its own weight falling.

IN THE BEETHOVEN YEAR

More than any countess with white wrists
(a pretext always), it led him on as years
went by, the black hulk gliding always
open and ominous, further out of reach.
He could not see what drew it. The conniving smile
hinted at filthy sidings and the boom of cannon.

I live in a glass cage. A man in white
wants me to sit up and catch the sounds he tosses.
He is mild, inquiring, concerned. The sounds are delicious.
I snap and fumble for them. The glass fogs.
They whistle past unnoticed; they are gone,
clamoring to each other in the ionosphere
forever like white souls in hell.
                                        When I look down
my wrists are free. The wires to my head don't hurt.

My dear, it's no use. So many words have snapped
for us. It will be over soon. Don't listen.
Look at my lips. I bring you silence. Sleep.

CHANGES

I.

A minor revelation:
when the scales fell from his eyes
Bartimaeus took one quick
look at the nearest observer
and wanted them back again.
(Some miracles are impossible.)

II.

I will get small and hard.
I will tick in the night by your bed.
If you try to kill me the snap
of my shell will break your leg.

III.

I took off my house. I became
a cloud. I took off my mind
and branched like lightning.
I forked and rooted in you.

I took off my clothes. I kept
the two coins in the pockets.
I put them over my eyes
and tried to take off my body.

Instead I spent them both.
I've lost my voice from buying
and selling. My eyes have tunnel
vision. The sight's on you.

You say you are getting smaller.
The first word I learn is good-bye.

IV.

The solution is there. It is cloudy.
I want your leavings. Give me
scraps of paper for flowers,
snippets of wire for crystals.

Break my bread.
Give me crumbs.
Give me memory.

V.

The whistle blows. Two strands
of paper spiral down.
They heal themselves together: serpentine.

They separate. They wrap
bulkheads, shouting throats.
An eruption of paper buries
the port. The ship sinks.

WILDFLOWERS

After three weeks apart
we drove for three hours
through a drenched Texas landscape

and though you held my hand tight against the gearshift knob
and though I stroked the loved meander of your ear
we talked only of our daughter.

But in sixteen years I swear I never saw mesquite so green.
Even its thorns
must have been silk.

And the tall grass stood shocked, or hunched over,
its stilled cascades
baled green, steel-bound.

Everywhere were those wildflowers
that come so seldom
their names are all forgotten,

and over and over you braked, stop after courtly stop
                    on the dingy cinders of the shoulder
to let me gather
each vital color.

I laid them on the dashboard, cut stems wrapped in tissue,
                    drenched in water from your desert canteen,
where they rested
to my destination.

Minutely diademed grasses, oxblood clover, cyclamen-veined
                                        mallow with melting petals,
paintbrush pagodas of coral and cinnabar, meadow aster, mint
with square sentry-box stems —

all still at hand
in a plastic motel ice bucket
punched out, leaning hard to keep their heads up.

I too. Across half a continent
our trajectories met
from Dallas to Kilgore, a willed collision of shooting stars,

leaving behind
this silent shower
of gentle colors

that will be gone tomorrow
as you, today, are gone
whatever once flowered between us.

WRECK (FOR THREE VOICES)

for Ann S.

"Whatever you do, it's gonna cost you plenty.

Dear, we have driven so far, a terrible way,
All morning, she said, she couldn't concentrate.

"The body work alone, banging out the damage,

it is no wonder you are drowsy,
She finally let her assistant do the babies.

"takes God-knows-how-many hours.

no wonder we sprawl drenched
It was gratifying that four of the six Apgars

"Then you got to consider, this here's an older model.

in mutual sweat. My neck muscles clench
were definitely subnormal, as long as you didn't

"The color's not standard either. Special order.

at the shock of this dim fragrant day
consider the appalling implications.

"That *and* the parts. *If* we can make them fit.

as if after whiplash.
If those women only knew! "The physical signs,

"But fix it up and you got what they call a classic.

With tears and soft words NOW *I wrench*
"although subtle, are unmistakable, once the syndrome

"Only don't leave it out on the street once it gets finished.

the slack wheel from your spent grip, crash
"is identified . . ." Some weasel shadow prowled

"Keep it in the garage, don't let nobody drive it

our two lives at stalled top speed ONE RING ONLY
nearer and nearer the nest . . . ONE RING ONLY

"but you, or your insurance won't pay off.

into the lethal metal and concrete glare
"Good God"—she hung up—"and I call myself a scientist!"

"And yeah, I know, I'll kinda miss it too,

of unmendable woe. Those crushing, cherished needs
But the terror wouldn't slink off. Finally she couldn't

"the way it is now, especially that bandanna

snap, shatter jaggedly free.
stand it, *had* to go home, *had* to be sure;

"you got the bumper tied on with.

Silent, I stroke your intact, lost body, maimed
and in panic, backed Funny Yellow smack into a lamppost,

"Christ, lady, how should I know? Maybe forever.

invisibly. See how my blood-grimed fingers gleam?
a mere two weeks after all that expensive work.

"And like I said, it's gonna cost you plenty."

BLACK STONE

Over and over I walk
this beach, and over and over
pick up black stone after black stone
filling pockets and hands, trying
stone by stone to empty my mind.

A starfish big as a child
sprawls by seaweed and crabshells,
a mesh of flies lashed to its windward side,
its radiant, tunneling sphincters all dead-ended.
Today, too, there is coral
flat-lobed as blanched
juniper leaves, some edged
with the indigo blue of the deep.

And no black stone is all black.
And no black stone is the same.
They are chopped and veined with white, ideograms
I cannot read, though I want
to speak the truth today.
We have met again, we are friends,
though my mind keeps on conniving against that simplicity,
as the sea lays its weary bets upon the sand,
its strategies transparent,
its face a guileless, wrinkled lunar gray.

Black stones, earth cinders, digits
of witch-mermaids burnt and sunk
in the hushed, obsessive glossalalia of water,
you are all lost.
                    This hand
is a stone that will never lie in his, and the years
we might have spent together wash away
behind us now.

RUBATO

Mozart spoke for the strict left hand: in common time
four stalwart unwavering sixteenth notes to each beat
of the tireless broken-chord Alberti bass,
the notes rammed accurately home, deep-driven stakes
of some sturdy functional enclosure

for mobile capricious melodies to live in,
as geese, those exquisite, homely fowl, inhabit
their pens, moulting gossamer handkerchiefs.
At the goosegirl's rude shout, they may pause for an instant,
heads tautly raised, in sinuous choral unison,
their round throats throbbing, their feathers lifting and shivering
with each strident, delicate sigh.

There is that other pause in which the heart,
its entryway flooded with airless black blood,
falters, engorged and helpless, and meditates
an instant upon its own death.
Wrapped in a filigree of veins, a timeless
blind-faced hunter's watch abruptly shaken
and set going again, it races to catch up,
rattling out spates of flustered seconds,
strings of jet beads that break and scatter.

Tenuously, tenaciously living
through the lapses and fugues of one heart's inclement mercy,
a fierce hesitation possesses the wakeful mind:
the tormented scramble to the topmost bars
of the Great Ape House, *that* pause, there, the one-handed
dangle, the crowd-pleasing rictus, the metronome swing,
the leaden, inevitable fall, the final abashed
padding off, exposed and shielded
by the sore, red-rumped escutcheon of desire.

A flexible measure, both lingering and abrupt,
quivering like a breath-shaken flame,
Liszt wrote of Chopin's *rubato*, adding that women
understood it better, as they did all things
relating to sentiment and poetry.

Those countesses played as they danced: a vertiginous pause
at the crest of the second beat, white draperies lifting
then settling, chins coquettishly tilted above
the vulnerable long throats.
How each woman dazzled, her radiance for the moment eclipsing
her dark companion, though she might lose herself
in *the shiftings of his azured yearning.*

Time stolen or broken, the fustian Abbé
wrote, telling for once a complex truth.
The goosegirl bit down on filched instants, testing their worth,
then hoarded them under her featherbed, until one day
she found the eiderdown slashed, the treasure gone,
the ruin, the ruin, of seconds, seconds, a lifetime!

Pearls blush on the old countess's knobbed fingers.
Even now at some memory the thin breath lilts in her throat,
catches and breaks, as if before a kiss
or a sob. Before death. Lightly she shrugs the shoulders
no one cares to uncover now. Women
indeed *are* better at it.
The word means *robbed.*

(The italicized quotations are from Frederic Chopin, *by Franz Liszt, translated by Edward N. Waters, Vienna House, 1973.)*

WINTER CLOSING

It was you who made the rain and the fair weather.
A body that the largesse of fever leaves
is itself, only itself, so small a room
to live in, the grave seems great.
                                        The fountain is empty
where last summer, whirling in plumes of water, the children
splashed and settled like little birds, a sundial
this mean reminiscence of light has frozen
perennial at blank *now*. Leaves, erased
from smudged sky, bare scrawled reiterations
of limbs like a childish punishment: *we are maples,*
maples, maples, and trefoil and cinquefoil,
lie in drifted labyrinths the downright keyhole shape
of feet obliterates, but cannot solve.
At the stagnant verge of the lawn, the conservatory
glistens with its equivocal rainbows of orchids
like a bubble caught in an oil slick. Incendiary,
the false heat sears the throat like chalk dust or quicklime.
Astringent and overweening, chrysanthemums
in the cold room flaunt rank on rank their omens of fortune
and longevity, fading lunar into that dusk
where cramped hours end, like white lights boring
into the deep shaft of night, as the gate clangs shut behind.

SE

II

"...INVISIBLE"

MARE'S MILK

(the Countess Sonya Tolstoy, musing)

Fresh from his first cure "I,
aged, toothless fool
that I am, have fallen in love,"
Lyovochka wrote to his aunt.
Declaring himself to me
in cipher, he traced
initials in chalk on my parents' card table.
"Your youth, your thirst for happiness . . ."

I guessed the rest, and knew that I must love him,
and tried, and did.
                                        "Her terror. Something morbid.
She knows all."
                                  I knew nothing.
"It is impossible," he wrote
"that all this should end except with life itself."

Nine years later "You looked old,
too thin, and pitiful"
he wrote, away for his second cure,
of the picture I had sent.
A kerchief covered my head, shaved bare
when I tossed delirious from childbed fever:
our fifth, a daughter, all still living then.

"My friend, great writer of the Russian land,
return to literature,"
Turgenev, his great friend,
dying, wrote to him.
Gorged on sun, mutton, fermented
mare's milk, worn out with riding, in his skin
tent, did he read, did he answer?

Back from Samara, he visits
muzhiks on their deathbeds, rages
when a son plays joyful dances on the piano.
Incurable, he lives his life on paper.
He has no words for death.
He will never answer.

I have written little and badly, interrupted
by children, nursing, noise.
I am ridiculous
in his eyes now, and know it.
Some nights, switching my coarse hair by the embers
alone, I think of the mares and the strong women
who brew their pungent milk in leather sacks.
I see the moonlight stroke their bold flanks,
their proud heads. They bear and nourish all,
never resting. All is distance without them.

They lie down only to die.

("Mare's Milk" is an impersonation loosely based on the Tolstoys' letters and journals, and on Henri Troyat's monumental Tolstoy, *Doubleday, 1967.)*

CENDRILLON

So bright, says the prince, you could scarcely see her. Beautiful,
he says, and means that she had more wings than winter
and hid her face in them, but he sensed her heart
beating, beating away in its lucid sheath
like the sun through a burning glass.
She had fixed on him; inflamed, the prince must have her,

and harries her down even into her blackened corner,
his heralds baying love. This bumpkin girl
with her scullery scowl — is it she? He is not deceived,
Prince Bonhomme, the literal-minded; the slipper fits.
Let her wear it, loaded with gauds and lauded by trumpets,
in constant pomps proclaiming how he won her,
this prize, this personage, this monument
who once was clear and sole as a drop of water.

What might have lived, he wonders, had he left her
brilliant and comfortless in her own ashes?

EDITH ASCENDING

Veering among the fireflies, two constant lights.
Loud among the cicadas, a harsher rasping.
Only I was awake to see the American lady
and her gentleman friend arrive. Swaddled in white
linen head to toe, wearing goggles in utter darkness,
through billows of dust and moonlight they ascended.
Our sleepy songbirds woke and mistook them for morning.

We offered them anchovies, cheese, oil soup.
Then their driver, even at that hour,
saw to his rubber-shod mount, and stroked its flanks
till they shone again. At last all slept.
                                                            But at dawn
she was up, demanding to see our poor child
in his wreath of dusty grapes, and our startled mother
flaking sweetly from the chapel wall. By the gate
the automobile once more stood snorting and fuming,
shy at the edge of the cliff. Its fifty headstrong
horses, it seems, were made only for climbing.

We had no bells that morning. With twenty men
on our end of the borrowed rope, we swung them down,
tolling the slow switchbacks one by one;
till the road eased, the pine boughs resumed their hushed breathing,
and the strangers were saved. Perhaps all miracles
happen so: sweat, noise, exorbitant demands.
Still, such a fall might have had its own beauty.

Often I think of the *Signora*.
Who holds her back now?

(This poem and its companion piece, "Edith Cast Down," owe their lives to R. W. B. Lewis's Edith Wharton: A Biography, *Harper & Row, 1975.)*

EDITH CAST DOWN

Summer afternoon. They lift me at the window
to see my garden grown again. One awful week, years ago,
my cook was flung from his cycle, his neck snapped;
and my footman, poor crazy sympathetic Romano
shot dead by his jealous wife, the local *cocotte*
who, in a word, boiled over.
Then came the sudden wind, wrenching and tearing,
that filled the parterre between the boxwood borders
with a potpourri of salad greens and roses
and left my cut-leaf maples both dismasted.
At dinner that night, there was an unseemly pause
between the entrée and the roast: the second cook
lay senseless in his blood on the kitchen floor,
an eel seethed in red wine. I was not, of course,
informed until after the brandy. All that is seven
years ago already. New maples sway in my window.
They close the blinds. I am lifted to bed again.
My hand moves in a foolish benediction.

"So here it is at last, the distinguished thing."
He was deceived, my dear Henry. For two months
the unworldly stranger loitered on his threshold,
and each long day he was lifted, as I am,
to his window, to watch the ships, toylike and far
on the sullen Thames, and the white fog coming.
La pensée ne meurt pas . . . can that be true?
Thank God we never wasted him, not then,
not now, though he is gone twenty years.
In the buzzing heat my cypress rock at anchor,
my mists are of lavender. How long,
after all, have I been dying? I loathe
this undistinguished lingering. No window
can ever open wide enough. I want
the limitless spaces.

MANTA RAYS

(Kaupulehu, Kona, Hawaii)

Night after night
on the same circuit
they come, cruising the shallows,
the shadows, haunted by plankton,
to the soft swish and lull
of water beneath this floodlight.

Binocular to excess
their eyes look away from each other,
duelists who have paced off their distance
and now stand back to back
preparing to fire.

The rest of their heads is all mouth.
Like immense sugar tongs
lined with silver and pearl
two cartilaginous mandibles
clasp the water we see as vacant.

In feathery washes
of ink and blurred charcoal
they bear on their broad backs
the nocturnal markings
of moth or barn swallow.
Yet their bellies are all noon and sand.
And their tails, vestigial afterthoughts,
whisper *quirt*, *stiletto*, *shiv*,
wounding the yielding swell.

Dark sails that the water enters,
fills, and propels,
they swim, straining light.
Their bodies are all undulation:
rolling, unrolling
white boneless wing tips
against the porous rocks
like rug merchants displaying their wares,
or, in the black distance, setting
pale triangles flapping like storm warnings.

What invisible lines
hold them tethered here, weaving
on the heavy current,
wet kites
rubber seraphim
for whom moving, feeding, breathing
are one?

SLEEPING ALONE

Poor scrap of fur
about to be tucked away
in a scrap of silk
slashed from a too-long dress
I wear, deluding myself into prettiness,

to be coffined in a sleek white plastic box
that formerly contained
eight shades of frosted eyeshadow
all unflattering,
why am I so overwrought by your tiny death?

Is it the bit of litter stuck to your stiff nose?
Or the way your lifelong companion, eager to greet
and grieve with me, bounced slew-footed
over your dry light rumpled body
and almost raked the black wide-open eye,
still brilliant and soft as a garnet or a ripe currant,
with the talons of one slim hind foot?

Now he plays prairie dog
in his corner, shunning both of us,
holding before his yellow rodent incisors
like an old lady touchy about her bad breath
a fan of cardboard sheared from a garish cereal box

which he masticates with electric efficiency,
as when both gerbils, in the good times
before Topper's smashed hind leg
before Champ's ulcerated, bleeding belly
gnawed each day's junk mail open
for the lost both of us.

Now Champ the Gallant Gerbil
lies dead by the community property tennis ball
that he and Topper, with the tireless stupidity
of long incarceration, heaved over and over
into their food dish, or rammed up the climbing tube
to their lofty plastic latrine.

Yet like the fuzzy sewn halves
of that tennis ball's cover
they fitted themselves together
each night for sleep:
Topper both pillow and mattress,
Champ the unbudgeable, oppressive comforter.

Wakeful, from a bed as big as a ping-pong table
in a white lace robe with nothing under it,
I have come down to consort and condole with you, widower.

For who now will splint your gimpy leg with velvet,
and what wounds can you wear like roses over your heart?

A GIFT OF DRAGON COMBS

What hybrid chimerical
beasts are these, wearing pleated
waterfall snouts like pug dogs,
brows ferociously umbrella-ribbed
over wistful simian eyes,
sporting flaming streamlined crowns
of chicken hackles?

The mismatched furniture
of their faces must trouble them:
inexplicable cabriole legs
with, beneath, an abandoned truncheon,
and a slatted, excruciating hammock:
fangs, unretractable tongue, linked rungs of the beard
unslung on fiery occasions.

Poor charlatans! Behind the flutter and bluster
of outsized kite heads
each hides a weak single span
of humped scales, swaying
on pinched lotus claws,
and a tail fluted, refined
as a clump of papyrus, or the headdress
of a veteran supermarket pineapple.
Thus dwindling, fraudulent, infantile,
indeed fetal, in their rages
as in their proportions,
(read from head to tail)
each pinned to a clear plastic comb
by a placental glob of epoxy,

what can they do but rant,
and offend, trying to stand
daily, their slippery ground
in the treacherous mass of hair
you were pleased, friend, to call beautiful.

So I call beautiful the resurgent fragrance
of sandalwood that has mocked
the hasty hand of the carver,
and escaped the slick shrouds of lacquer,
to offer itself to me now, an eloquent balm,
cousin to camphor, camomile, orris root

and all such simples as promise
no grand end to pain
but the homely scent of comfort,
the exact, strategic kindness.

EARTHWORM

Beneath root-tip stalactites
past ossuaries of pebbles
through the thin enlacing veins
of subterranean rivulets fine as human hair

he has tunneled
to blunder in a straight sprawl
across blind concrete, a snapped
drawspan blocking fully half a square

or a leaky pink garden hose
layered with tape at the middle,
humped folds of red skin
wound like a loincloth over the plum-colored gonads.

Streamlined at both ends, double-engined
charged with the energy of canceled reversals
he plunges due east toward wet grass
the slowest possible orient express

and the most adamant, his colors the stony
salmon, ochre, and rose
of the legendary city of Petra
whose very name bespeaks rock.

The tense and dilatory motion
of his spring-loaded anatomy
is fraught, too, with the tardy elasticity of rock
collected and releasing
along faults made explicit
by unfolding deformity.

Yet still I have not told how he moves:
no whiplash meanders, no sinuous indirections
for him, but rather a straightforward two-phase telescopy:
a wrinkled and tightening hunch into himself
then a blunt, bunched thrust, his smug unthwartable

snout persistent and gross
as a thumb in the soup. And yet
in his leisured digestion of distances
peristalsis becomes dance

while he goes on and on, confiding, tireless
endlessly extruding himself into the future.

HAWTHORNS, LATE SPRING

I.

On the brittle abandoned limbs
of the aging hawthorns
a furious rash of bloom
breaks out again.

A year ago I showed
my daughter how each seeming flower
on its glossy divan
of frilled green leaves

was in fact a cluster
of rosettes, each little
as a child's nipple and of
the same intimate pink.

How easily those flowers
perturbed by a squirrel's attack
or the probing fingers of wind
tore loose, fell, shattered —

monotonous prisms
through which all the morning light of the brilliant world
broke again, again, and only
into the same voluptuous paired colors.

II.

It was water, its chill, agitated
lunge toward mass, toward fixity
mercurial no longer,
but dense, granitic, glistening,

that sundered the tuning fork
of one winter hawthorn,

snapping branch from branch like a wishbone,
stilling the ancient wind-struck keening.

Trying to decipher
that burnt-out brush stroke
dashed down on fresh-laid snow,
I wished back those piebald, volatile

jets and washes of green, as I stroked
a violated wooden fountain, warm as flesh
to my chilled fingers, cream-colored,
broken in fresh rills and reaches,

the flow of its growth stopped.

III.

From crotch to root in the ripped
grottoes and votive niches
of the hawthorn's lofty wound,
incongruous shelf fungus

piles its homely brown crockery.
Thus out of the deaths of friends
we grow, or so one new
friend tells me this spring;

who tells me, too, how in the human brain
the nerves of the two hemispheres
entwine at the corpus callosum
bridging opposites, as the branches

of plane tree and hawthorn
span my narrow street again
with ferocious pinks and greens;
as I welcome each morning

the autumnal blaze of their colors.

STINGING NETTLE

Its disguise resides in the commonplace.
The ancient, shabby needle of the fields
plies its trade among blackberries, under dock,
or apes the sprawling pungency of mint.
Stalks upright, leaves opposite, toothed, of an attenuated
heart shape, its flowers loll in pendulous racemes
so little showy they seem an irritant,
like lint or a fallen eyelash.
Dioica, incomplete, of one sex only,
they inhabit, like Godwin and Wollstonecraft, two houses
to express the furious rectitude of their separateness.

You know the rest. Under the microscope
the leaves and stems bristle
with narrow metallic volcanoes.
Brushed, they erupt in poison, invisible, adamant
as unrequited love.
                                        But should you, in rage
and pain, crush the offending
branch, the blood of the nettle will surely heal you,
just as, scalded, the spiteful shoots
turn tame and nourishing.
                                                  Further, the caterpillar
of the ravishing Admiral Skipper
feeds only on stinging nettle; and perhaps the butterflies
too are immune, and return
each summer in frivolous flight like love letters
among the stern catkins.

One final warning. The plant is perennial.
Its roots multiply deep, in hiding.
Its pain, like that of childbirth, is strangely effaceable.
Forgetful, you may grasp it time and again
in an open field, among flowers.

SWEET AMARYLLIS

No amorous giant
could equal the length
that springs from this plain brown bulb
with the wrinkled skin.
Leaving nothing to the imagination
two censorious leaves
point upward from the base

at this tense hammerhead crane, wearing a bonfire
of flowers like a foolish bonnet;
this wildcat windmill, this phallus
decorated not with forget-me-nots
but with sizzling pinwheels.

Androgynous, you wear a nymph's name.
Wallflower, your pot too tight
and shiny for dancing, you lean
in the doorway, sweating nectar,
spilling pollen like face powder.

Half succubus, half angel, attended
by the wizard ginkgo and the uncanny
monkeypod tree, you appeared
to Linnaeus, wearing nine heads,
each furnished with a serpent's tongue.
Four voices, then, can never be enough
to sing your praises.

Amaryllis, sweet amaryllis!
Still, when you are mute,
let me sing how your long leaves
die back into the bulb
like sputtering fuses; how you lie
all winter in dry earth:

in your scaly heart, white and waiting,
an embryonic armada,
the translucent sails of its flowers
furled like umbrellas;

and how spring after spring you return,
remaking yourself
out of memory.

DARWIN'S MOTH

Darwin never saw it.
I can never remember its name.
It had to exist because the orchid existed:
Angraecum sesquipedale, loveliest
of the white, night-blooming orchids of Madagascar,
its trailing nectary thin as a knitting needle.

In those years I kept orchids
as lonelier women keep cats, but I never told you
that story, or the parable I framed about it:
the quiet presence with wrapped and folded hair,
the wide rustle of marbled or vellum-colored silk,
and the door closed gently to visitors
while the master indited the inconsolable postulate
another would prove long after he was dead.

How does a moth perceive a sleeping body?
Has it the smoldering residual heat
of a garden plot, that loamy, occult luminosity?
Are shoulders, fists, cheeks, felt as huge
knobbed buds, impregnably shut?
Why did it seek my face, over and over,
a frantic rush like scratching fingertips,
my skin some taut, frosted pane?
Cloaked in a stilled blizzard
of sensory hairs, wings white
as if ice-veined, what lunar flower
was it seeking, what perilous lily cocooned in snow?

Light calmed it to a tranced stillness on my headboard
where its moon dust lingers today.
For how many hours, as if with a dying king,
did I watch with it, offering it milk and the lees of white wine,
murmuring the chaste and furious music of its name,
Maenas vestalis?
You gave me the book that named it.
But I made these lines for a stranger
who turned to me in the dark beside white flowers.

CLUMSY GHAZAL

My friend says, "At least this one isn't hurting you.
But I wouldn't let him borrow your car — or your heart."

It was written that you would slip, fall, skewer your arm
in my shower. But did you have to bring me your laundry?

And why must you comfort, (platonically, but in public)
the heartsick wife of a homicidal black-belt?

Drunk, you wear your earring to bed. Next day,
a predictable, but piercing, earlobe hangover.

Your story: two boats collide. One sinks. The other
rolls over completely, then bobs up, righting itself.

The worst pain was knowing your socks were tattered and dirty.
You apologized. See, your grandmother was right.

Blood, women, calamity. Your other girl
wore a belly dancer's jewel of broken glass.

Hurtling toy automobiles spangle your Christmas card.
You almost lost your head to a telephone pole.

The petrified perfect red rose you gave me droops
but lasts in my toothbrush glass, stoned on Empirin.

Your friend's girl, still mourning Elvis's death, won't sleep with him.
How long must I wait for you to get over Janis's?

Meanwhile I go to the zoo each day to see you:
slim feet snared in barbed wire, eyes unfocused, luminous.

COLUMBUS

There is no formula to capture
the ribbed curves of a ship.
A man on an airplane
told me that once.
I trusted his telling
with my life and my daughter's life
and after our bags came, past midnight,
I drove him to the landlocked town
we both hazarded as strangers.

In the shipwright's shed, they lay
each rib-line winging out
from the beached spine of the keel
— not the wood itself, but the piercing thought of its sweep
and gleam — staked by hundreds of shining spikes.
I forget how the timber is bent
to that skewered, flawless shape.
So cartographers slice darts
in the ideal gauze of circumstantial seas.

Ships are operatic, notorious;
can ground, like the heart, anywhere:
as the compass rose of a frost-stunned oratory,
the kernel of mounds of pink jasper.
But I believe that man
whom I never saw again,
and would squander worlds
to see the haughty timber of your beauty
arrayed on the flood for me.

COLD ALBA

There was snow yesterday.
What did it mean, felting the air
with a nap of little prisms
that clog, grounded,
into cold fur about the feet:
ermine, lonely divine
right of queens?

This poem is called *alba*.
What makes the electric leakage
of weeping cells that home as lymph
to the heart, or
the closed drench floating the concept
of an egg's autistic
universe?

Seen right, fog's refractive.
Maybe pinpoint angels dance to
the slash of micron semaphores?
What warms best, we
can't see: ice fog, forsythia,
barbed crystals of honey,
frozen milk.

THE MASK

I.

Age gave her wit, at least,
that woman whose name you won't tell me
whom you swore never to see again.
You won't say what she wore, how she tuned
her guttering beauty to the glare
of your strong unhidable throat, your fencer's waist,
that night when, at her whim,
you wore to the ball the mask
of an old man.

I must imagine for myself
the furrowed translucent plastic
baldly high-domed, absurdly fringed
with ragged synthetic wool,
under it your real hair
glimpsed dark and shiny as unborn snakes
beneath the nacreous leather of the egg sac,
and at the narrow eye slits
the consuming blue of your gaze,
Greek fire sequestered behind stone.

A straightforward, mordant imposture:
she could be me, you can still
become anyone.

But what, but who
lies behind the story, behind
the story about the story, behind
this replica of duplicity, unmasked lines
tuned to the stress of your beauty,
your pain?

II.

You will never notice when you put it on —
a thing small, light, forgotten like a crumpled handkerchief —
to grate and chafe under your ordinary skin, invisible:

the remembered splendor of your arrogant maned head
the remembered languor of your violent blue eyes
the lost collusion of youth, beauty, desire —

that its gossamer weight may oppress you
its threads sing through to the bone
will not concern me then.

This mask I made to leave you was my mirror.
You will wear it simply, and always,
as in time we all must.

Look through its eyes, to see what I now know
when I am gone
before you have to go.

HAWK OF THE DESERT

The grinding of the expensive metal tumbrils
that brought him here, bound, blind, and under sentence
to almost-freedom, stops. Loosed, he soars
above the hunched plumage of burnooses,
the tame gold beaks of coffeepots.

What comes to light is not
unlike his boreal home.
An expanse of glare, a same
embrasure of sea between headlands.
He reels, circles. His feathers
are heavy. He scans for snow;
for the jotted black characters
of eye, beak, claw, that betray
white creatures to his hunger.
He is cold for the heat of prey.

But these are beneath his notice.
They scurry out of sight
into warrens of baked sand.
Nuzzling for flints, for potsherds,
their trowels twitched like noses.

He avoids them.
As, always, the wild
and obstinate water evaded
its masters; coiled, slipped down
lightly, past painstaking cataracts
of stone set to contain it;
and now in the shade of a thirsty aqueduct,
sulks, hisses, tantalizes.

*(The hawk of the poem was a white Greenland falcon.
See* Looking for Dilmun*, by Geoffrey Bibby, Knopf, 1967.)*

BAIT

Wild pet I fed from my plate
someday as you pace the dung
and fetor of your self-made cage
your right tamer will come
with hand more deft and ruthless than my own
to bait with choicest condiments of rage
the delicacies you bite at and spit back.

Even the damask penetralia
of the lady's slipper orchid are bait.
In its sugary, spike-sided tarn
whatever ignorantly craves, crawls, waits,
is flung to drown, one more wrong capture
in a world where there is scant appetite without deceit
and the spite of the used, using back.

ARTIST AND MODEL

Unknowably stupid, stupidly unknowable clothed,
she becomes real on her dais, taciturn, bare,
wintry, fallow. And he must coax spring
from her imprecisions of gooseflesh and matted hair
somehow, somehow. . . .
                                        Impossible, yet so easy!
The crayon lengthens a haunch, corrects a breast.
His eye and hand, her body become one lazy
confounded tightening toward anguish, toward rest.

He pictures her image (*his* image!) infinitely multiplied,
a reflected fire in the manifold stare of the dark.
She dreams of her young lover's silver seed,
yet lies open to him with the spilled abundance of apples.

He thinks how only direction and velocity change —
how desire, like wind, is everywhere and immortal.

THE PRICE OF ADMISSION

He is a toll taker in a temple of art.
He measures the passage of time by the price of admission,
twice now what it was when he first entered
his glass kiosk, half orgone box, half telephone booth.

More people took taxis then.
In the sculpture garden
the ruminant bronze nudes caught the light
and tossed it back all day, exact change.
The soul of a petty bureaucrat . . . he has grown a mustache
above his tamed mouth, and wears
the visor of his cap pulled down hard.
But sometimes he catches his own panicky eyes
peering back from the glass surround, the eyes of a man
caught forever in a revolving door.

At night, acid and the meticulous burin.
Its handle fits his palm like a ticket punch.
On the veins and scars of the zinc plate, his eyeshade
casts the green light of an unattainable forest.
Sylvan, sylvan . . . again the child is crying
whom they named for two great saints of Russian literature,
and his thin wife pushes her food away uneaten.

The sculpture garden has shrunk to the length of a boxcar.
In it the plump Maillols huddle like refugees
and the sun sifts down in ashes.
                                                            After the fire
the empty, charred frames went out like coffins,
a bearer at each gilt corner.
Once it cost only a dollar to enter.
He was young, about to be famous.
Above him, invisible,
were Giacomettis slim as little goats
and the water lilies' unblemished platters of light.

THE FACTS OF LIFE

for Katharine

The body is not on your side.
While you are trying to sleep, or writing a poem
in your head, it shelters the shadiest
activities. In the attic
they show blue movies
and on the ground floor
is an establishment whose interior
is red, dim, plush.

Commotion in the bordello!
The doors swing wide, the walls of the place are shaking.
A mob of customers barges in.
It is clear they are all villains,
so many abstract twitching mustaches,
so many leering eyebrows.
They riot, yet all goes swimmingly.
But one skulks behind the portières.
He looks for a hidden door.

You would not like the madam.
She is fat. She lolls in an antechamber.
She doesn't come out for the party.
She pouts. The truth is she never
wanted to leave her sisters.
But the skulker finds her magnetic.
He's a plunger. He loses his head.
Spiderlike, she swallows him.
But he doesn't die. They are
beside themselves repeatedly,
chromosomes clinging and cleaving,
genes kissing their doubles.
This goes on for months.

The bordello becomes a machine shop.
It is a growth industry.
Overcrowding ensues.

In another scenario, the floozie sulks alone.
It's an off night. The customers
find the atmosphere poisonous.
One or two take a look around,
but she isn't there, or she's wearing her hair in curlers.
The place isn't what it used to be.
Trash it! Tear down the curtains,
rip the red paper to shreds,
yank the stuffing out of the pillows.
It all goes out with the garbage.

Each time, you are the informer,
the outraged moralist, the vice squad.
The body? It only wants
to make you happy.

THE BLOOD WEDDING

Rain. They have had to come in
from the garden. The bathroom door won't lock.
In the kitchen some strangers load a tall coffee urn.
Above, fiddle and dulcimer, the thud of dancing.

How to walk, a little bowlegged, skewed forward
in the big gleaming shoes, the unfamiliar
rasp of nylon tugging the hair of her shins?
It is like a logger's tackle made white,
limber, miniature, still treacherous:
slung to it, the little mattress, its hammock ends,
its coverlet constantly soiled and needing changing.

She turns out the light on the brimming bathroom sink,
its tangle of shame, soaking.
Her mother is dancing, more strangers kiss in the stairwell.
They came all this way to be here.
Used and wrung out, the roller towel on the ferry
was blotched with the red of many indifferent mouths.
She couldn't walk there either, the ship was swaying.
The dancing and the kissing will never stop.

HYDRANGEA BLUE

Water angels, I wrongly thought them,
orotund in blue tinseled light.
And *water* is right. The reedy stems taint at first frost
with the bronze of monumental fountains.
But the factual *angel* is a vessel or basin,
the antique catchment, the Cytherean scallop shell
that bore the halts and plunges of its fleshly passenger
across tart spermy foam, under white skies.

Who painted those flowers?
I forget, I ask it again
each time I enter a faraway guest room
where stagnant rain-colored mirrors regard each other
and the frizz of dead ladies dozes under intricate ivory.
Her watercolor is historical where we long for anecdote,
its paper foxed, scorched, insistently smoothed.
Ocular *and* oracular, the crystal bowl bulges
with diligent wonder: how drowned rubber stems usurp light.
Her leaves flock and preen but are biteless,
a generalized plumage salvaged from lilacs.

And the flowers, nothing to be said of or about their null-
colored avoidances, neither loose wash nor scandalous impasto,
but that they lie:
that from life, hydrangeas are varicose
as the thighs of mothers of many children, violet
as the torn-across ink of love letters, blue
as the rapist's battering, bruised knees,
red as the blood-dolphin's lunge in his laboring throat,
gray as the small chilled corpse in spring,
its lead foil eyelids, on which unimaginable noon
looks down in anguish.

Not your mother, your great-aunt.
Yet what, since, was so lovely
as her sky, before it learned blue?

POPCORN, COTTON

My daughter, who eats nothing, eats these.
Little vortex, spitting powder puffs,
I haven't yet noticed the direction of your spin.
Is it counter in our hemisphere, clockwise south?

How many strata of plastic in my kitchen
— Bakelite to Teflon to Lexan —
are laid down upon the antediluvian basement rock of Formica.
And lo, a beloved dinosaur is herein revived —
popcorn, weightlessly lumbering,
streamlined to anorexia, a mere
! ! ! 23 calories to the heaping cup 23 ! ! !
once relieved of the poisonous generic unguent
that lubed the porno dreams of puberty.

Cottonseed oil, probably.

My fantasia slides upon this pivot:
popcorn or cotton, the same magic about it,
white knuckles *and* card fans in one unfolding trick.
Beneath a ripening sun, cotton bolls widen
and flare with a dainty-jointed pop,
flowers still in bloom on the same bushes,
bridal white with a bitable flush.

In the prettiest cotton field I ever saw,
two rows out, two in, it didn't occur to me
to ask the whorled floss which way *it* spun,
nor to question the luck of the farmer
who soon on a Glorious Fourth when
a spanking wind did snap and startle to panicky
attention himself, his good horse, his proud flag,
would feel all bolt skyward, his white Stetson
flung forever out of the ring
that rallied round his reddening banner.

The plastics in his household now serve Jesus
who alone comprehends all odd nourishments
catapulted from the finned turbines of the natural.

LIGHT SUMMER READING

You couldn't fool him; Symmes was an insider.
If the expedition lashed on to the Pole,
they'd top a snow dune; the dogs would disappear
like a caterpillar over the rim of a cup.
He knew it; he turned his mind out like a pocket
with a linty detritus of stars inside.
It was *here* hollowed out, and if he hadn't seen it,
he'd felt the furnace blast of the hidden sun
prickling his soles when he strayed from the weathered boardwalk
while the ladies shivered in their bathing machines.

Lawson blew on the dust; it scurried away
like the stars falling out forever. So all creatures,
as: tides, light, blood, excreta, odysseys,
cyclones and feathers, lovelocks, liverworts,
obeying themselves, churned loose and found their proper
density. In his genesis, Suction and Pressure
made the engine go, stamping whirlpools on his fingertips
in passing, while the universe gulped and sucked.

Fort held no fixed opinions; watched the others
coming and coming forever upon love
by infinite paths, as on a Möbius strip.
A risible man, but when he hurt, God bled
sunsets and northern lights. "We're property," Fort said.

(See Fads and Fallacies in the Name of Science, *by Martin Gardner, Dover, 1957.)*

WALLENDA, FALLING

He is falling asleep in a snug cave of speed.
The window hives slide canted to his passing,
packed with a cellular, honeyed light so ravishing
that the sage toes crimp with pleasure, the body furls
with fetal sweetness into the ballistic air,
while the sharp chin tilts in a fledgling skew toward the collarbone.

His stick is umbilical, skillfully fisted to
the chest like a chinning bar, struck and twanging with tension.
And still he falls, into the loss of his long swaying,
knees flexed against the premonitory least gust.
His lips part and curl in a greedy, breathless unsaying
of the sinews' cryptic skill, the encoded steps

now straying, straying, ingenuous in space
as his eyelids fall shut, fall free, nostalgic, virginal.

BRUISE

Try, he said, his tomatoes
a perfect pyramid of mounded red.
He held three splayed in the nicotine-
cured fingers of one wizened hand,
and while I was thinking *pawnbroker*, *Atalanta*,
the other, quick as a cutworm,
tried the ripeness of my buttock.

I was young then, he offended
and frightened me, but I bought.
I thrust out my own arm, leafed and shady with currency.
The tomatoes, at home, were lumpy and bruised, I would not
eat, but turned them out, still sacked and dying,
into the garbage.
                    Today on the plane away from you,
I felt sore, I could not sit still, the silk chafed my breasts,
while the fervor of your grip seeped leisurely up from bone
to the surface skin of nipple and thigh, to the stung
black corner of my upper lip.

Love never used to bruise me, nor was I then
so lighthearted. Literally, I now think
Baudelaire meant those lines, *her body . . .*
bruised like a peach for the sake of wise love.
He was writing about deceit. But what honest joy
comes to me now as hunger, consuming, passing.

CALM

Calm. I have become
very calm. I mean, you could say
anything to me. I would not scream or cry or
on the other hand fall sighing into your blissful arms.
I don't see any arms, even yours, as
blissful anymore. And what is more
I doubt that it matters whether I do or not.

All this sounds like, but isn't, misery.
There may be a lot to be said for a loss of the elasticity
that let one (me) go on and on loving and hating,
rejoicing and being sorry —
all those overtones, undertones, resonances, harmonics,
those sky-borne arpeggios of the nervous system —
that now have become a simple *ostinato*,
its few repeated tones: work, child, friends,
food, drink, sleep, the little and larger luxuries.
Or all these tones in one clean blast of white noise,
jammed on *send*, the monotonous network anthem
primed for annihilation at any moment.
Sound like a beacon, like a lighthouse nevertheless,
bringing new others to stay becalmed with me.

Yes, but how did I get here?
Well, through a time of things
banging about, falling or being broken,
through a long time of such things and of much
incomprehensible shouting
and weeping, and of the kind of sleep
that feels like drunkenness but is really exhaustion.
All that, you know, maddeningly interspersed
with flowers and money and the incomprehensible
elasticity and heat of other bodies, blast furnaces,
I thought, where the spirit was forged,

since I believed then in the spirit and its trials,
which are believable when housed in lovely bodies.

I wouldn't have it back, I'd as soon stay here
as long as I can. For one thing, when the wind
turns again, there will be only
shortness of breath, long howling, bones breaking
of their own accord, things and people
going or being poignantly borne away
or trying gallantly to stay, to stay on, to hold on to
more things and people, their use or significance vague
and steadily vaguer. And the same
with the baggage of one's own self;
this uncaring is no doubt the beginning
of a long losing out, as if one left behind at each hostelry
some cherished garment or jewel for the maid, for no better reasons
than that the suitcase was heavy, the excuses for adornment few.

Still, we're not there yet. For now there is this interval,
this phony peace, in a neutral country between betrayals.
I'm not sure if you're staying or passing through or if
I trust you, and least of all sure you understand
why I'm trying to speak of the storms before and behind us
and present, even, but dormant, like the workmanlike gurgle
of coiled intestines, or the old baroque notions
of heart and mind still inwardly drowsing
like cobras in baskets, so tame and sleepy
they could no more lift their hooded
heads, than I could raise these five
passive storms, and then five more, to hold your face.

THE TOWER

Rousedfrom god knows what wine-soaked after-dinner
sexual fantasy, staring mad-eyed
from my spinner's tower with its twelve-paned windows
at the warped lights in the lake, the shuttling freeway
edging its undoing, a dream from my daughter's young childhood
came back to me, a dream I took then
for an omen of destruction and war.

They — we — were walking, a man and a woman were walking
on a gracious thick-sodded lawn, walled at one side,
which then began to sway, moist and green and unstable,
to swing in the early throes of seeming earthquake.
Then to heave.
Giving birth.

The man and woman looked up,
looked backward,
— they were already walking away —
and saw behind a monstrous, cut-stone tower
— yes, archetypal, and silly, too, as tall
as six stacked World Trade Centers,
each of its razor-edged, mitered granite blocks
a story thick, and piercing
its base, three wide-arched, thin-walled tunnels,

so that the building's whole weight, the millionfold crushing
force of it,
bore down on pillars with the narrow span of a girl's waist,
and the tower, that moment awakened to its own impossibility,
had begun, from the crenelated battlements downward, to sway,
itself hypnotically disrobing itself, divesting
monolith by juggernaut its millennia of unreason.
Each stone, remember, the size of a sizable hut,
and falling with the undodgeable plenteousness of hail;
breaking up, however, in tumbling flight like meteors,
though these frictionless falls cast no light.

I recognized the couple:
Adam and Eve from Masaccio's *Expulsion*,
at home in their fig leaves among the brutal Florentine
juggernauts;
and felt them break into, at most, a trot.
Did I dream, or am I now inventing
the feel of the thud and slide of their jogging hips
and shoulders bumping, cold with the sweat of fear?
And something not fear. But delight.
In the touch. And something else. The green
smell of the velvet lawn, being broken and flung
skyward, great divots, spinning gardens.

And I too could smell the sweet earth,
its wet mud and torn grasses, the severed lace of its roots,
as the clods hurtled back to their gouged and tumbled
resting places.

That innocent smell!
In a life that is all duty and no love
and not of my making, I often try to imagine
it, and that the man and woman survived.
I would like to think they ran far enough,
ran far enough and were lost.

FOOLS THE EYE

(after teaching during Artfort week at
Fort Worden State Park, Washington)

Houses are being dished up beside fried chicken.
Most students don't notice until I ask them to,
in class, next day. I say one doesn't do
sonnets as one does hair, or museums. Plots thicken,
indeed, but offstage. My plot involves the stricken
sweet eyes of some Texas steers, white hulks in blue-
est night, and like any good alibi, seen through,
in that case, a trailer-house window. I won't say *broken*
of the state that brought me there, but maybe *bent*
to want some vast to set my small scale to.

In the dining room here at the fort, there are like blue
glass gaps in the muraled walls, where the real fort looks in,
nocturnal, through its whitewash and green day-face. On this view
let eaters ruminate: how a locked-out other may glisten,
O heart, through carpentered holes in depicted skin.

BARBAROSSA

But you didn't kiss me.
Though what we were doing
was at least as good
as dancing. I kept looking out
at the harbor, the stilt-legged, red container
cranes lovely as a flock of flamingoes
and thinking, *Now, now.*
As before in the locked-up bar,
with jungle wallpaper reflected in its stagnant mirror
and the little dance floor quiet as some pond
cluttered with duckweed, pollen,
shed dragonfly wings.
No liquor to be had anywhere. You smoked instead.

Now there is this hulk,
curb-trained to its hawser
riding high on the huge, continuous surge of its bilge pumps
like a racked ship in a bottle.
Inside, I am sure, there are rats,
splintered teak, moldy grain, bits of brightwork,
a sprinkling of archaeological gold among ribs.

You didn't.
And you didn't.
Ships ought not to work for a living.
Romanticism has nothing to do with cargo
— my child, your wife, your children, my craft, your work,
the charting and plotting logistics of adultery —
and everything with the choiceless pathos of wandering.
In spite of its grandly comic and phallic funnels
there was something paralytic to the shape
of our stowaway ship. Albino, shadowless,
its high, diminishing bulk stretched backward for blocks
when we drove away in your car.

The thing is, bilge water is lovely as any fountain,
playing, playing. Flaked steel can sing like a drum.
The thing is, you can move it,
move them, *those deadweight tons, with the flat of a hand.*

So I looked up the great Barbarossa, an Ottoman admiral
in the century before his empire declined to piracy.

MOSAIC MAN

for Anne

I. An Accident

Not *quite* the gilt stone confetti of sanctity:
concrete meridian, windshield, the high-speed plate tectonics
of bone in the sleeve of scalp, the glove of face,
a contained, battering velocity
that leaves the skull crazed as a fine
china darning egg, candled by CAT scanners.

And there is still that fertile blot of rage
that holds, and flares out like a smudge pot
guttering lecheries, guttering blasphemies.
So that in goodness, patience, wonder, you may think
of your enemy's
soul, your husband's soul, as a fleck of blue
delinquent fire, dancing gleeful above
the steady, undetonated length of the spinal cord,

and thus avert all thought of the factual specks
of bone in the watery cushions of his brain, grit
on which that briny glutton mollusk
grinds, battening.

II. The Confidante's Ditty

One to sing me sad songs,
One to tell me lies,
One true love to betray me,

One more who tried,
And one to turn from me in his great pride.

No one
The one.

One to give me music,
One to show me fame,
One to father a daughter,
One to engender shame,
That same who murmured stories till sleep finally came.

Not that one,
Not . . .

Self-lovers, self-tormented.
And self-haters, self-satisfied.
Yet there was one dear man who loved
A lovely boy, but tried
To love me in the long grass when I would have died.

And every love had all my love
And each had none.

III. An Animal Model

In a cellular *tour de force*
with roots in both science fiction and heraldry,
researchers quarter and quarter again
the tiny genetic escutcheons
of mice of clashing genealogies,
whose rifled and tidied blastocysts

are then, *like* quarters, slotted
into a lineup of cool, brooding bellies,
to tumble out at term as jackpot litters
of multi-syncratic nature, shenanigan-
skinned, with bias-cut

cowlicks.
Well, *I'd* like

one of those, Anne, only human.

IV. Some Pieces Placed

A madness, a frenzy, relentlessly growing —
in his last years, his women became so many, so many
it could not have been some one *he craved then,*
but some thing — *or perhaps only the nothing that finally*
claimed him.

Just that. Nothing.
Not peace, certainly.
Although to you, who had lived for so long estranged
and withdrawn
in a nun's smouldering passion of self-sufficiency,
he was abruptly gentle.
Death
must have felt like a cool hand, a cold compress,
some welcome, chill way out of his driven fever.
She

was younger than I, but not beautiful.

You saw the last once only, not at the funeral,
where you would have welcomed her —
Yes, welcomed!
you assert to the commiserating night nurse
who sits with you all through one long blue
worrisome November afternoon, piecing lives
and deaths together.
And you are the youngest
in the taverna's company of widows
brisk in your American tweeds, tragic star
to a black chorus fallen silent
over empty cups at adjacent tables.
Well,
it is *fascinating,* he *was fascinating. And she —*
how lonely she must have been, night after night
— no, morning after morning rather, for he never slept easily —
a late shadow, or an echo of myself,
needlessly furtive, believing herself shunned.
There in the corridor after he died, I would
have held and wept with her, but the hypocrite doctors
kept her, somehow, away —
just that one glimpse, rounding a corner, flanked by white
guards. And I may have heard
her: above that theatrical
glottal sobbing the Greeks go in for, there was
one thin, homing bat note
keen as my own silence.
Poor child, poor child . . .

Poor friend, who writes this letter.
There is a wedding of widows on your page.
What else is she to you, this woman whose tawdry
dazzle blinds, whose unknowable edges rasp yours?
What touches you in her but the spliced and grafted

cells in the one flesh of unimaginable love
that your lover craved, and died for?

THE PRESS POEM

for Scott

Sometimes it does not want to run.
Cogged mastiff, it glowers in place,
its fleetnesses erratically,
inwardly churning.

Or it becomes hysterical
grasping and wadding
sad tangles of paper
with clinking hydraulic fingers
as its gauges veer toward burnout.

And it is both passerine,
franchised and domestically smutty, between
hamburger joint and muffler shop,
and grandly peregrine, dangling
from a groaning Huey over printless Ketchikan,
yet suffers, ubiquitous,
the huge, brooding pathos of endangerment.

For the arachnoid robot encroaches, and the thrashing spew
of the high-speed, high-pressure ink jet,
before which this omphalocentric and foolishly
pacific animal stands helpless,
whose many lives have bent to one end only:
that its flighty ratchets and wing nuts, its congregations
of gears both cylindrical and helical, its spinning, horizontal
diapasons of great and lesser copper rollers,
its grand baths of fixatives, reagents, emulsions
and all its tremulous harnessed tonnages

may whisper with the wistful delicacy of eyelashes
across the supine nudity of paper.

THE LINGUISTIC COMMISSION REPORTS FROM THE INTERIOR

Unlike our country, where the words
are small, succulent, and docile,
theirs, wiry and mean,
must be cornered and battered with rocks.
Even then they may break loose, snapping and foaming.
Their least bite can fester.

The adverbs are especially menacing.
They circle the tents at night,
making sleep impossible,
though hammocks help a little.

The nouns, nocturnal and clumsy,
are sluggish by day, hence
easily ambushed. In
captivity they breed copiously:
five hundred variants of "want,"
a thousand nuances of "hunger,"
each stringy, foul-tasting.

Small wonder the natives chew air
constantly to numb the pain,
washing it down with a brew of stinging
nettles that resembles *pulque*;

or that they cruelly cast out to die
old orations, epigrams, homilies
— even the small-beer mutterings
and yelps of love —
though they might, with care, have lasted centuries;

or that their most sacred object
is a blank piece of paper,
their epic poem
seventeen hours of silence,
their highest virtue, panic
in the face of hyperbole.

LIEBESTOD

(suggested by a promotional film
for the French Mirage III fighter)

X marks the spot. The girl
spread-eagled on the beach, oiled and glistening
in her bikini, breasts
hard handfuls like grenades. Beside her blanket
a revolver and a transistor radio.

The pilot can't believe his luck, swoops low,
the surf tickling his wingtips,
and scoops up the sight again like a greedy pelican.

She sits up to watch him gone.
A fine haze of mica veils her sunburn.
She doesn't wave, but her sunglasses
dazzle and burn like phosphorus.
                                                  So at the top
of the steep loop back to her, he flips
his canopy away like a champagne glass,
ejects,
            and hits the beach, legs pumping
as he hurtles strand after strand of barbed wire,
racing to reach her in time
to salute, whip off his pants, and yell
"A votre service, m'am'selle!"
as his jilted plane goes up like a bunch of roses.

The earth does in fact move for this conjunction.
A tide of mortars rolls in
and a hot heavy rain picks out their movements
like an expert knife thrower.
Far off the alert missiles quiver
in their hardened silos, and the red telephones
croon to each other like bowerbirds. Over the black
waves, clouds of bombers dip and sway
damp-winged, the false eyes on their wings
blindly flirting. Here at last
is love to set the world on fire.

KINGS OF ENGLAND

(after a collage print of handmade, hand-dyed paper, one of a series by Akiko Shimamura)

Look as you will, you cannot find the kings,
their textbook faces canceled behind silk screens.
The house where they hang is old. A rude old lady
must take the tickets, explain the art and furniture.
It's decrepit-looking because it's old.
                                                            It isn't.
Mere months into ragged newness,
its collapse is faked, what luxury!
Then it's homemade!
                                          She beams, thinking pies,
or the scrimped cloth mosaics on other walls.
She understands those. Her cramped hands know about upkeep,

and this work, too, is rags newly construed.
Rope can be pulped veil-thin, an orchard drizzled
untasted into tints to enliven no one's breakfast.
Fiber *is* moral. What we call currency
passes, unsteadily tiring, from hand to hand,
a whole fickle gamut of dying falls,
and means its value no more than the old woman
means foolishness, bruited like thought from hand to hand,
from mind to mind.
                                          The mind that thought this hanging
pulp sawbuck the size of a coffin
is middle-aged, beneath child-fine frizzy hair.
It belongs to Akiko. One scathing voltage passed
through the artist, fist-sized, in the eyelid-red dusk of the womb,
and grounded, a supernova announcing nothing,
yet leaving her alive to spend her life
and Hiroshima's light, on us.

THE ARMED MAN

The armed man is sleeping. Above his head
planets gleam in the borrowed apple light of stars.
Who can plumb his slumber, steeped
in the stirred and poisoned syrup of numberless intrigues,
or fathom the thumps and eddies at his few
cranky motion points, occluded as they are with iron?

He cannot lift himself or tender
so much as a gauntleted finger to kindness
without offering the winking gap
that tempts blade or bodkin.
Wrist, ankle, throat, the bellows slits between ribs:
what flexes is hazard. He has turned drowsy
turtle to cheat alarms.
                                        For should he move
it must be with the integrity of hatred
that launches stone-sling and scythe-sweep,
brute impulse made impenetrable by haste.

The armed man still sleeps.
Around him the debonair meadow
leaves its wavering, light-struck legions of grasses undrilled.
It is one brush in the hand of many painters.
The will of each painter would leave the light unshorn.
The will of the light is to seem the hair of champions
unarmed and harmless to hold the field forever,
brightest of armies unfading and unfallen.

Lullay, lullay, armed man.
But what if he woke and were angry?
The idea of orchard would crush to flayed pulp
and core in his jointed fist, the notion of meadow
slit, tangle, and lie trampled,
a rippling token of silk underfoot.

Ah, but what if he woke and were happy?
If he heaved the visored iron turret
from his shoulders and looked up dizzily
into the staggering wealth of branching constellations
ripe and ripening forever beyond his armored reach,
and opened both gauntleted hands
toward the fruit's ungraspable, unappeasable fall?

THE DREAM OF DANCING

for Rebecca

I. Student

She has dreamed the dream of dancing. She is happy
though she knows that athletic, aerial life, like hers,
is subject to fatigues, impacted enmities,
intrigues and scuff marks, skipped stitches and grime.

She remembers, even, certain special hazards:
the oaf with thumbs thrust into her kidneys, lifting,
the sacrum sacrificed to a dazzling upward
swan dive, and in each fiery heel more grating
delicate bones than anatomists admit of.

The dream itself comes often with burned-out footlights,
or ends ignobly in tethered levitation,
head thudding against the ceiling, wingéd hands
pinned in cobwebbed corners, or the leap aborted
and the spun toe skidding askew in its concrete box,
balked by the abstract interment of gravity.

II. . . . and Teacher

She reigns in double splendor in her salon,
this only slightly post-Diaghilev personage:
once framed between the claw-footed rosewood grand
and the stringless gilt harp by the door,
a young swan in cascading cerements of moonlight,
or a stopped, peregrine goblin, the explosive tattoo
of her frail crossed wrists stilled,
fey, deathless girl before whom
the brute hunter's crossbow falters;

and again, shrewd bird receiving, in a purple
satin Empire armchair, wearing Milanese
and Seventh Avenue civvies, clearly reveling
in her plush tough lilac velvet, her peach silk,
the succulent buffed leathers of shoes and handbag,
and the heft of gold chains shelved on the brittle collarbones.
Her tiny chin's out-thrust. Each elegant
arthritic hand reposes on a white toy poodle.
And the auburn hair is *pastel,* to use her term.
But the legs she crosses are slim and taut as a girl's,
and her velvet skirt is slit to draw the eye.

And no one knows, and no one needs to know,
the dead grandbaby waiting in the Beirut airport
crated like spoiled fruit,
or the slow, leached beauty of her own bones' decay.

I couldn't do an arabesque . . . novocaine!
Can you imagine anything so silly,
gone in two hours?

Or the *sotto voce* hiss in 'the litle girl's room'
at Galatoire's:
He hasn't drawn a sober
breath in fifty years, you know what that's *like.*

What he said was something else.

We walked everywhere in Paris,
all day, every day. And do you want to know
what she wanted to do all night?
Every *night? That woman?*
Make love, that's what!

That's what.
The sedentary guest has gone. The stagy
living room is dark, silk-curtained, cavernous.

The plaster egg and dart join hands, the chandelier's
prisms wink and tremble. Fringes sigh
as the ancient macaw stirs beneath the floss-
embroidered flowers of the Spanish shawl
that drapes his cage, and rasps his one hoarse greeting:

Goodbye!
Goodbye!

And who can say what dream
each dreams alone? Tomorrow, may they rise
to joy, in their habitual bodies.

SESTINA: SERAPHIM

Consider the technical difficulties of the sestina.
Consider the practical difficulty of Seraphim.
For years I've waited for the right idea,
one with a mystically perfect division in six
clean segments. I doubted that it would come to me, ever.
Now it has, I see the world in a new light.

Indeed I see the world itself *as* light:
workaday bodies tremulous with a Sistine
splendor of form and color, which may be the Seraphim
agitating invisible wings, or the idea
of wings, between us and the ruddy facts of six
P.M. and autumn and leaves that we will never

know green again, cocooned for an instant, forever,
in a pulsating membrane of celestial light.
But back to the practical difficulties of the sestina.
Its crabbed, tedious form demands seraphic
patience of reader and writer alike. Ideas
cramp and harden beneath its belligerent insect

carapace, setting innocent truths at sixes
and sevens. What honest poet ever
felt anything but dismay to see the delight-
ful flesh of the visible world lashed to the sestina's
hacked, procrustean form? Not even Seraphim
can mend the strewn, unsalvageable ideas

in its demented wake. And to salvage the idea
of Seraphim themselves, we must not ask how six
of anything, paired or tripleted, can ever
function at all — but see them in the light
of impossibilities (like troikas or sestinas)
blessed, rarely, by some inner benevolence. Seraphim

(take it on faith) can fly *and* hover. Seraphim
soar closest to the flame of pure Idea.
In the celestial hierarchy (nine, not six
Orders) they have the ear of God forever.
Their wings are fiery cataracts of light,
laving even the cloddish feet of the sestina.

Behold now the earth-bound, limping, six-fold, seraphic
Idea of the Sestina aloft in light,
silly and deathless, amen, forever and ever.

MIDAS

The despicable elements of his life survived,
the ones he either couldn't touch or wouldn't:
scullions, major-domos, plenipotentiaries
back from alarming embassies; seneschals
and huntsmen, farriers, furriers, and seamstresses;
charwomen, varlets, helots, his prime minister,
a sorcerer or two, and the palace dwarf.

The first few were marvels. His favorite cook, for example,
bent double beneath a boar's head surrounded by thrushes,
the platter alone worth a year of barbarian revenues
(he'd had the bad luck to wobble); not to mention
the exquisite verisimilitude of the notched
birds' tongues, the boar's splintered tusks, the pucker, swell,
and ooze of the gold-leaf burn on the cook's right thumb.
Then came a gardener, toothless, offering pears,
the queen (she'd grabbed at a pear), and his old nurse
with perfect gadroon borders of tears down both
sides of her nose (he'd thoughtlessly wiped one away).

The later groups were hilarious. He'd thought
it wise at first to have them all stacked in the treasury
to be melted down in case of war or inflation.
By then, of course, the able-bodied were mostly
frozen, golden. Urging on the stumblers
he'd lost (or gained) a number of them forever.
There was, in addition, an excessively numerous
but touching family group, come to retrieve
a son for burial, but whether out of grief
or avarice, he would never know for sure.

Then it got worse. He passed through hunger and thirst
to permanent horniness. Loneliness was the worst.
The few survivors gibbered at him from galleries
and antechambers. Above the clatter of metal
leaves, and the ripe grapes chiming like little bells
from the arbors, he could hear the elusive whisper
of clothing, flesh. Each silken or raucous voice was a siren's.

Then he thought of the ones he'd lugged off and hidden himself:
the golden girls in pornographic poses,
the boys with polished Hesperidean backsides —
even a cunning goat with lost-wax curls.
He had draped them all in out-of-season tunics.
His lust and shame made monumental sculpture.

And now, you think, it's time for the happy ending.
But Dionysus begs off. He's no soft touch,
for flesh once lost to art is lost for good.
We leave the king forever as we found him,
in the rich glare of his punishment, dazzled to blindness
by appetites he can neither hide nor die of.

EXAMINED LIVES

for R. H.

"Thai food tonight? No probably not, but yes
it's not too late, bring your friend."
Between sun and rain, between winter and spring, in a skittery
wind, we ascend the slanting walk, its bland
concrete inlaid with shards of celadon pottery.

The wind-chime birds in tinkling migration are brass,
the beveled bricks glass, in the entryway.
Inside on the humpbacked black grand
(a Kawai), a couchant leopard lies sentry
alert of sheathed claw, sharp ear. There are buttery

tulips, and fire-blue iris, a beheaded trumpet
of amaryllis wed to its Favrile double,
and the tight-fisted climbing, hand over hand, of urgent
stock and snapdragon, a splurge on the dining table's
monastic oak length, robed in ikat.

Here is white wine in a brace of cobalt goblets.
And here is Coke in a jelly glass for the host.
And here is Smog, the almost perfect pet,
in the company of babies and children, choleric,
but in that of poets, doting; doting most
on the most allergic.
So I can't say canine love is not to be sneezed at.

In back of the sofa — is the trumpet motif involuntary? —
a whole Chinese village marches in bronze procession.
The living room plants are turned and glazed like pottery,
while one lily-shaped vase flares open beside my kneecap.
Though it's almost worn out, the clivia's
flamboyant orange fanfare is tucked by the leopard's oblivious
left, ebony ear. By its paw sits a votive teacup,
Imari, gin-filled, someone left there while playing Cole Porter.

And here is the stainless steel fireplace, machine-tooled coffer
where the veriest gem of a fire would be outshone.
On the cocktail table, three black lacquer boxes offer
their golden anachronism, the Thousand Cranes.
Down the hall is a bathroom with tilework grouted
like graph paper,
eight Tivoli shower jets redrawn by Mondrian,
and a stepped-back sink in the form of a Deco skyscraper.

And so to the studio, passing a village of kilims
encamped on a leather couch, disguised as pillows.
Pierced like colanders, two shadowy Balinese deities
haunt the bittersweet wall, looking down on a guardian dromedary
and the myriad gold-ringed drawers of an apothecary
chest, chest-high, and stuffed with yellowed secrets.

Not much in the way of equipment: clamps and pliers,
a polishing wheel — is that silver dust on its gritty
surface, or merely the common household variety? —
bone needles, a soldering iron, different gauges of wire.

"This is the only way to test for amber.
Heat some sharp tool, a hole punch, a blind awl,
then work it deep. The real is tough and pungent,
the false, though as richly colored, is scentless and limber."
The visiting poet watches, a blond owl.
The resident poet lifts a lapis unguent

jar, then lays it near a mother-of-pearl pod
with two pearl peas inside — some scars are pretty.
The telephone is ringing across miles
of loss. But here a necklace lies dismantled,
or maybe merely unfinished. These mahjong tiles —
she clacks to make him look, a bit disgruntled.
"— saw it first in the paper myself. Out of the city
on business, since last month. They'll fly the body

"home tomorrow. He'd not been well
for a long time. Fevers and chills, antibiotic-
resistant. Tests for every sort of exotic
parasite. No, no, not that. Though he was afraid
of it, of course. These are dark days, dark days.
Services? Not planned yet. You're good to call."

He speaks in the calm, clipped tones of a newscaster.
She doesn't really hear, then hears too much,
and sifts her beads, now counters of disaster,
though only one has died. That lovely poster
of a nude male back — they are, incredibly, discussing it,
the phone hung up again, the social veil
intact and swiftly drawn. This is a visit

after all, about art, among artists.
She passes to the bedroom now:
familiar blue Imari, lacquer, scrimshaw;
a platform bed, a casement corner window
restated in the many-tiered vitrine
before its many panes, in which serene
small cats, and little Buddhas, sleeping rabbits,

buttons and clasps, enamel finger sheaths
rest breathless, timeless pause in the huge breath
of storm and sun outside, the muddled day
where skeins of golden rain and cherry blow
and settle, brown and lift, are borne away,
souls flying. Such a house here, such a host!

Lares, penates, so beautiful and so many,
calm intercessors who are always calling
like living friends and lovers, dearly bought
and dearly held, and falling, always falling
to cherished pieces from the too-fierce grasp,
what gods are these? And we, and where awaited?
One guest wears the surgeon's red ribbon brave at her throat,
in the perilous first days of a longed-for pregnancy.
Our host is a gay widower, this day created.
And one strung this scatter of words. Here, let them clasp.

PROTEUS

My master liked to play tricks. He'd toss
a shaggy blue paw at the shore
and when he jerked it back like a clumsy conjuror
there'd be mullet jumping, or a ransom
of unspent agates, gone with the next wave.
Little things.
No matter how hard he tried
his heart was too vast, fluid, and cold
to cram into one body.
I'm more volatile. I think now he told me
what to do out of jealousy.

Like any craft, it was hurtful and crude at first.
How I struggled to throw the combers on, a pelt
that seldom fit.
I blush to recall my juvenilia:
the three-legged bears, the tailless crocodiles.
My audience didn't notice.
Even then they complained I didn't communicate
though the tongues of my whole zoo rattled like clappers,
though by then I had perfected
all my little tricks of dentition
and my bones — this is prophetic! — functioned like slide rules.

Just when I got things right, they said I'd retired.
But I went where the work was.
The modern world offers too many theatres.
The price of art is anonymity.
Nobody recognizes the aberrant blip on the oscilloscope,
the unexplained ghost on the late show,
the alarm in the peaceful house.
The times are against me: consider
those cereals more permanent than marble.

The work now is sterile, exhausting,
all bit parts and banality;
those hideous lives of agar and centrifuge —
as if simple replication were ever enough!
I'm a classicist. I liked
roles I could sink my teeth into.
And only my vacations, being sunlight
on a Dutch wall, or a hatch of Monarch butterflies
by an abandoned railhead, have kept me
— I can't say whole — but going.

I'm at the top, now, of my forms
and I'm staying put.
I am anything I choose
though you're too slow to follow
while I run through all my frequencies, visible, invisible
with the rippling grace of a dancer at the barre.
Virtuosity has its hazards. Faster! Faster!
My sine waves snap and hum like rubber bands.
My peacocks and my coelacanths melt together
into that bureaucratic blur your dulled eyes,
scanning twelve plodding times per second,
mistake for normal
mistake for yourself.

But I know, I warn you, where I am going,
and my great speed steadies me.

THE TEN THOUSANDTH NIGHT

Prince, this is my last story. Listen
to the din that screams through clenched teeth into your ears.
Feel the hot grit scour your eyelids, and the force
that lifts and whirls you through thinnest air to the uttermost
edge of the world, effacing all inscriptions,
as the djinn's furious breath sputters and stops.

This is the last oasis. An obsequious vapor
hovers above the sandstone spines of palm trees
and their hacked, bedraggled foliage. Restless among them,
behind them, grimy silhouettes you guess
as camels, cattle, hinds, black goats, pass
and repass, their fabulous colors crushed to dun.

The hidden water jangles like a miser's purse,
and you enter the last palace. Erected this instant,
or coalesced, it has been here always, crumbling,
or heaped up again, a dune formalized.
Pass, prince, through the intricate portals that clamp shut
as the glittering passages pale and narrow, while
the dust you walk turns ever whiter and finer,
desert skin no sun touches.

Now gloat over your last treasures: corroded chests
brimming with the mild rainbow eyes of victims,
the stolen glare of diamonds; and lamps to whose spouts
you lean without touching, listening
for the voices of murderous wind, and the vast
conspiracies of shipwreck. Scuttle over this wealth
and fall, drowned and gasping, into the final

room. You are marooned in hollow glory
carved by a giant tongue. The grandiose spiral
of your life narrows to thirst. Before you, veiled,
the last woman waits, salt-white, wavering,
a fountain of tears grown old beyond all fiction.
And now the clever hasps of her heart spring open.
My lord, you are enthroned there, tiny, gorgeous,
expectant.
                    But I have lost all my voices,
however many dog-eared nights remain.
Prince, it has always been the same story,
and always it ends in death.

HANNAH'S QUILT

Your first name appears once only
the year three times
(once upside down).
Before me lie spread
the literal fabrics of your life
bright-hued and durable
smelling of cloves and trunk dust
still wearing the gores of an outgrown skirt
the silk-bound sneer of a cast-off buttonhole.

And here are your creatures
and concerns, single and multiple:
your rooster, a cataract of fancy darning,
the cow and her calf, a red-stitched bovine madonna
and child in a sky-blue and white
plaid gingham meadow,

paired snowshoe tennis rackets
six bashful daytime stars
blinking green and gold, roused
from their reclusive twill and flannel beds,

and by threes, these:
stitched or appliquéd coffee cups
vinegar cruets identically sprigged with basil
and paddle-shaped straw fans
themselves strewn with raffia flowers.

I hear the creak and thump
of rocking chairs on a veranda,
the lilt and abrupt stillness
of wind cooling down in the live oaks,
and mockingbirds calling out
through the wind at beautiful random.
Fanning yourself, you rock and gossip with friends,
your painstaking gaze at rest on the blue distance

where a small boy
with rolled-up sleeves and trousers
bare feet and a straw boater
tilted forward to shade his peeling nose
walks, incredibly,
a cat on a leash.

That night you tucked both safely,
tiny and nonchalant,
to rest in one of your midnight-blue borders
watched over by archangel butterflies
taller than any mother or father
wearing swallowtail wings embroidered
with carnivorous spots and stripes.

You quilted Sunday-best fans too,
spoked fabric wagon wheels, halved.
In one of these, between wedges
of patent-medicine wild-cherry broadcloth
lie stern pillars of blackest watered silk,
even the rich best
of deep loss put to use

to turn the eye to other black fields:
one patch shaped like a listening ear
wearing the crescent moon and its watching star,
another a wide-shouldered oblong
where red and white roses
bud, bloom, and shatter from one tangled stem.

So perhaps the trowel-like
leaves of comfrey
the featherstitched coral fungus, the toothed whorl
of an unfolding fiddlehead
were planted nearby as remedies
by the practiced, cherishing hands of your two friends

who left as well
depictions of a few specimen plants:
one morning glory, fawn lily, thistle,
a single green pear,
unique beauties stitched as talismans
to charm the terrible fecundity
of your life, its obsessive
tides of fuchsias, marguerites, roses —
those unimaginably many roses with round
crumpled petals and pincushion hearts
so like passionflowers — to rest.

The year was 1892. Across decades
your red, steel-bitten fingertips brush mine.
You left the smallest prayer behind, shy
almost to furtiveness
— oh Hannah!
your forget-me-nots —

which I answer with one of my own.
Bless, Hannah, the work of these hands.

ACKNOWLEDGMENTS

Antioch Review	"Wildflowers," "Hannah's Quilt," "Kings of England"
Bakunin	"Cold Alba," "Artist and Model"
Chowder Review	"Hawthorns, Late Spring"
Grand Street	"Wallenda, Falling," "The Swans of Saigon"
The Iowa Review	"The Prize"
The North Stone Review	"The Press Poem," "The Mask," "Fools the Eye"
Ploughshares	"Darwin's Moth," "Hydrangea Blue"
Poetry Northwest	"The Gardener's Daughter," "Sleeping Alone," "Blond Mahogany," "*Rubato*," "Wreck," "Sestina: Seraphim"
Prairie Schooner	"Bait," "The Dream of Dancing," "Columbus"
Seattle Review	"Earthworm"
The Southern Review	"The Tower," "Clumsy Ghazal," "Bruise," "Popcorn, Cotton," "Barbarossa"
Telescope	"The Blood Wedding"
Water Table	"A Gift of Dragon Combs"

"Hannah's Quilt" was reprinted in NO KNOWN PATTERN: TWELVE POEMS © 1989 by *The American Voice*, Louisville, Kentucky.

Frequencies was composed in Intertype Baskerville
with handset Baskerville Foundry display type
by Donald M. Henriksen, Scholarly Typography, Salt Lake City.